A TEACHER'S GUIDE TO
Using the **Common Core
State Standards** With
Mathematically
Gifted and
Advanced Learners

A TEACHER'S GUIDE TO
Using the **Common Core** **State Standards** With
Mathematically
Gifted and
Advanced Learners

Susan K. Johnsen, Ph.D.,
Gail R. Ryser, Ph.D., and
Susan G. Assouline, Ph.D.

A Service Publication of the

Copublished With

LEADERSHIP IN MATHEMATICS EDUCATION
NCSM NETWORK
COMMUNICATE
SUPPORT
MOTIVATE

PRUFROCK PRESS INC.
WACO, TEXAS

Library of Congress Cataloging-in-Publication Data

Johnsen, Susan K.
A teacher's guide to using the common core state standards with mathematically gifted
and advanced learners / by Susan K. Johnsen, Ph.D., Gail R. Ryser, Ph.D., and Susan G.
Assouline, Ph.D.
    pages cm
Includes bibliographical references.
ISBN 978-1-61821-103-3 (pbk.)
1. Mathematics--Study and teaching--Standards--United States. 2. Gifted chil-
dren--Education--United States. I. Ryser, Gail R. II. Assouline, Susan G. (Susan
Goodsell), 1953- III. Title.
QA13.J66 2013
371.95'37021873--dc23
                            2013023466

Edited by Rachel Taliaferro

Production design by Raquel Trevino

ISBN-13: 978-1-61821-103-3

Prufrock Press Inc.
P.O. Box 8813
Waco, TX 76714-8813
Phone: (800) 998-2208
Fax: (800) 240-0333
http://www.prufrock.com

Table of Contents

Acknowledgments   vii

Foreword   ix

Preface   xii

Chapter 1 *Overview*   1

Chapter 2 *Adapting Learning Progressions for
          Gifted and Advanced Learners*   17

Chapter 3 *Assessment*   34

Chapter 4 *Differentiated Learning Experiences*   48

Chapter 5 *Management Strategies*   92

Conclusion   115

References   118

Appendices

    Appendix A *Definitions of Key Terms*   125

    Appendix B *Critical Readings*   130

    Appendix C *Teacher Resources*   141

About the Authors   148

Acknowledgements

Many people have assisted with the efforts in developing this book. They include the leadership of the National Association for Gifted Children (NAGC), the NAGC Professional Standards Committee, reviewers, NAGC staff, and experts who were a part of the development of the other books in this series on using the Common Core State Standards with gifted and advanced learners.

We would like to thank Paula Olszewski-Kubilius, NAGC president, and the NAGC Board, who have understood the urgency for responding to the Common Core State Standards and the gifted education community's need to have a voice in their implementation. From the beginning, the NAGC Professional Standards Committee also has been actively involved in providing the framework, expertise, and support for this book. Moreover, the NAGC leadership group also includes Nancy Green, executive director of the NAGC, and NAGC Association Editor Carolyn Callahan, who have supported the development process and the need for this book.

This book has also been strengthened through a rigorous review process. We want to thank these reviewers who took time to provide valuable advice and feedback: Scott Chamberlin, Toni Hillman, Sara Delano Moore, and Ann Lupkowski Shoplik. We also want to thank again the authors and contributors from the first book: Linda Sheffield, Cheryll Adams, Alicia Cotabish, Joyce VanTassel-Baska, and Chrystyna V. Mursky.

Finally, the authors want to express a special thank you to Jane Clarenbach, Director of Public Education at the NAGC office, who has provided the needed energy in supporting the authors through the process and a critical eye in editing the many drafts of this book. She has shepherded this writing project with great diplomacy, tact, and endless amounts of patience. Thank you, Jane.

Susan K. Johnsen
Gail R. Ryser
Susan G. Assouline

Foreword

Only a year has passed since NAGC's first two books about using the Common Core State Standards and gifted and advanced students were published. Urgently requested from all corners of the NAGC membership, the two books, one focused on mathematics and the second on English language arts, have been well-received by the NAGC membership and beyond. Although the 46 states that have adopted the CCSS seem to face a wide range of implementation phases and challenges—some advancing rapidly, others mired in state politics—the demand for guidance about the relationship between the CCSS and gifted programming remains strong.

That is why it made so much sense for NAGC leaders and subject matter experts to convene once again in Washington, DC, to consider additional materials to respond to feedback from convention attendees, state directors of programs for the gifted, and educators in the trenches. It was clear that something more was needed.

Although the first books help educators understand how to approach differentiation of student assignments under CCSS for learners who meet the standards earlier and faster, the two new teachers' guides to using the Common Core State Standards with gifted and advanced learners provide an even more practical orientation. The new books include additional examples of differentiated learning experiences (LEs) at key grade levels within specific strands of the CCSS. They also include examples of assessments that will be helpful in evaluating more complex and creative performance. Beyond providing additional resources, the books also feature a discussion of scope and sequence and how instructional practices for high-ability learners can be integrated in the classroom.

Clearly, the CCSS hold great promise for better teaching and learning, and they have stimulated a national conversation about what shape these improvements can and should take. With these high-quality, carefully crafted publications on how the CCSS should be implemented for gifted and advanced learners, NAGC has contributed significantly to this national conversation. These books not only serve as useful resources for teachers in the classroom, they also clearly demonstrate why grade-level curriculum and instruction are simply not enough to challenge our nation's gifted and advanced learners.

Testing, accountability, and teacher training seem to be the next frontier now that nearly all the states have adopted the CCSS. On that front, NAGC has a head start, thanks to these books. Professional development based on the chapters and examples outlined in these pages will equip teachers with the knowledge and skills to meet the challenges of the CCSS. As a result, the gifted community is well-positioned to successfully take the next steps with implementation.

We can't say enough about how remarkable it is that a key group of leaders and experts came together not once, but twice in service to gifted learners and the teachers who support them. The CCSS workgroup and others who provided input on the two books once again deserve recognition and appreciation, particularly NAGC Professional Standards Committee cochairs Susan Johnsen and Joyce VanTassel-Baska and their coauthors

Susan Assouline, Elizabeth Shaunessy-Dedrick, Claire Hughes-Lynch, Todd Kettler, and Gail Ryser.

The impact of this work on gifted education, classroom practice, and on the knowledge and skills of gifted teachers, as well as those who work in heterogeneous classrooms, will be felt greatly in the years to come. For the National Association of Gifted Children, there is no greater mission.

Paula Olszewski-Kubilius
NAGC President, 2011–2013

Nancy Green
NAGC Executive Director

Preface

Over the past three decades, national and state standards have been established for preparing teachers, developing programs and services, and designing curriculum for specific subject domains. Within gifted education, the National Association for Gifted Children (NAGC) in collaboration with the Council for Exceptional Children, The Association for the Gifted (CEC-TAG), has developed standards that provide guidelines for universities and school districts in designing coursework and/or professional development for teachers and developing services for gifted education programming (NAGC, 2010; NAGC & CEC-TAG, 2006).

More recently, teachers, researchers, leading experts, and professional associations have made recommendations for the design of the Common Core State Standards (CCSS). Built on state and international standards, these standards are aligned with college and career readiness expectations. Authors of the CCSS suggest that these standards are rigorous, evidence-based, and informed by other top performing countries (National Governors Assocation [NGA] Center for Best Practices & Council of Chief State School Officers [CCSSO], 2010c). Because most states have adopted these standards, they will replace former state standards and provide the foundation for the future design of comprehensive assessment systems to measure student progress. They will therefore have a tremendous impact on the education of all children, including those with gifts and talents.

In November 2012, NAGC copublished *Using the Common Core State Standards for Mathematics* (CCSSM) *With Gifted and Advanced Learners* (Johnsen & Sheffield, 2013) to examine how the CCSSM were adapted and differentiated for gifted and advanced learners. It was clear to these authors that although the CCSSM were strong, they were not sufficiently advanced for gifted and advanced learners. This initial book provided an overview of a variety of topics, including standards, assessment, research support, talent trajectories, collaboration, a timeline for implementation, and differentiated LEs. Given practitioners' strong interest in this first book and their desire for more differentiated LEs, the Professional Standards Committee within the NAGC initiated the development of this new book. Similar to the first book, work teams of professionals who have expertise in gifted education and math (or in English language arts or science) and were interested in developing the new books in each of these domains worked together in identifying topics that needed more in-depth discussions. They decided to include assessment, scope and sequence, managing differentiated curriculum, additional resources, and new LEs that were not included in the first book. This book is the culmination of the team's work.

Our hope is that this book provides classroom teachers and administrators with an understanding of expectations within a learning progression and practical examples of assessments, learning experiences, and methods for implementing differentiated curriculum in mathematics. We decided to develop a set of K–12 LEs within a single domain so that practitioners might use these as a prototype for planning LEs in other mathematical domains. We also included examples of assessments that would be helpful in assessing more complex, creative performances and in recognizing students who might have a particular aptitude for mathematics. Concrete methods for implementing differentiated LEs, along with the expanded set of resources, might also be used as a springboard for innovating more enriched and accelerated practices with gifted and advanced students.

Similar to the previous book, the authors firmly believe that giftedness in any domain is developed over time through interaction with nurturing environmental conditions within and outside the classroom setting. Students need learning experiences to develop their talents in mathematics. These experiences are particularly important for students in poverty, who might not have access to opportunities in extracurricular contexts. Students who participate in stimulating and challenging learning experiences may accelerate their trajectory, making it possible for them to achieve success with even more challenging mathematics. Practitioners should note that the recommendations in this book also might be used with learners who have potential to develop their motivation and interest in mathematics. Moreover, administrators and those involved with the implementation of the CCSSM may use this book as a guide for differentiating state and local school district curricula and assessments so that students who are advanced and gifted in mathematics have the same opportunities to show progress as typical students.

Susan K. Johnsen
Gail R. Ryser
Susan G. Assouline

Chapter 1

Overview

In this chapter, we provide an overview of this book and how the Common Core State Standards might be implemented with learners who are gifted and advanced in mathematics. Specifically, we address standards, differentiation, scope and sequence, assessments, differentiated learning experiences, and management strategies within the classroom, school, and district.

Standards

Within the past 30 years, standards have assumed an important role in schools. They define the important knowledge and skills within a specific subject area and provide guidelines for the development of curriculum, assessments, and critical benchmarks for students. Understanding the domain along with evidence-based instructional practices can help individual teachers establish a set of clear expectations and ultimately improve student outcomes. Common standards also provide consistency so that "no matter where [students] live, [they] are well-prepared with the skills and knowledge necessary to collaborate and compete with their peers in the United States and abroad" (NGA & CCSSO,

2010c). In this section, we will discuss the Common Core State Standards for Mathematics and their alignment to 21st century skills (Partnership for 21st Century Skills, n.d.) and the NAGC Gifted Education Programming Standards (NAGC, 2010).

Common Core State Standards for Mathematics

Adopted by 45 states, the District of Columbia, and four territories to this date, the Common Core State Standards for Mathematics (CCSSM; NGA & CCSSO, 2010a, 2010b) have quickly become the foundation for developing learning activities in mathematics. Designed by teams of math specialists across states, the new standards are intended to prepare K–12 students for college and the workplace. They emphasize thinking, problem solving, collaboration, and communication and are informed by research and reports from national and international studies such as the National Assessment of Educational Progress (NAEP, 2011) Mathematics Framework and the Trends in International Mathematics and Science Study (TIMSS) report in mathematics (National Center for Education Statistics [NCES], 2007).

In mathematics, two sets of standards are described: Standards for Mathematical Content (CCSSM-C) and Standards for Mathematical Practice (CCSSM-P). The CCSSM-C are organized by grade and secondary levels, standards, clusters, and domains. Standards define what students should understand and be able to do, clusters summarize groups of related standards, and domains are larger groups of related standards. For example, at the fifth-grade level, within the *domain* of Operations and Algebraic Thinking (5.OA), the student is expected to "write and interpret numerical expressions" (*cluster heading*) by "using parentheses, brackets, or braces in numerical expressions, and evaluate expressions with these symbols" and by "writing simple expressions that record calculations with numbers, and interpret numerical expressions without evaluating them" (*standards*; NGA & CCSSO, 2010a, p. 35).

It is important to notice that the standards and clusters may be related to other domains at the same grade level or across domains at different levels, forming a learning progression. For example, in measurement, students use measurable attributes to describe and compare objects, situations, or events at the elementary level; use measurable attributes in models and formulas at the middle school level; and explore measurement systems and measurement of more complex or abstract quantities at the high school level. Similarly, graphing is used to represent data in the Measurement and Data domain, to solve problems in the Geometry domain by graphing points on the coordinate plane, and to analyze patterns and relationships in the Operations and Algebraic Thinking domain by graphing ordered pairs on a coordinate plane.

Therefore, when educators are teaching the Common Core, they need to be cognizant of vertical and lateral alignments within the standards. Domains included within the CCSSM-C and the grade levels in which they are addressed are:

- Counting and Cardinality (K),
- Operations and Algebraic Thinking (K–5),
- Number and Operations in Base Ten (K–5),
- Measurement and Data (K–5),
- Geometry (K–HS),
- Number and Operations: Fractions (3–5),
- Ratios and Proportional Relationships (6–7),
- The Number System (6–8),
- Expressions and Equations (6–8),
- Statistics and Probability (6–HS),
- Functions (8–HS),
- Number and Quantity (HS),
- Algebra (HS), and
- Modeling (HS).

The CCSSM-P define the process skills that educators need to develop in their students (NGA & CCSSO, 2010a). The following practice standards are for all students in grades kinder-garten through college and careers.

1. Make sense of problems and persevere in solving them.
2. Reason abstractly and quantitatively.
3. Construct viable arguments and critique the reasoning of others.
4. Model with mathematics.
5. Use appropriate tools strategically.
6. Attend to precision.
7. Look for and make use of structure.
8. Look for and express regularity in repeated reasoning.

To develop innovative and creative mathematicians, Sheffield (2006; Johnsen & Sheffield, 2013) proposed a ninth standard: *Solve problems in novel ways and pose new mathematical questions of interest to investigate.* In addition to the practice standards, educators should encourage their students to develop a deep understanding of mathematics and aspire to become creative and investigative mathematicians (Johnsen & Sheffield, 2013; Sheffield, 2000, 2003). This outcome can be achieved by (a) having students pose new mathematical questions, add new ideas for solving problems, and create innovative solutions; and (b) having teachers ask questions that encourage mathematical creativity and use assessment criteria that focuses on fluency, flexibility, originality, elaboration or elegance, generalizations, and extensions (Chapin, O'Connor, & Anderson, 2009; Sheffield, 2000).

21st Century Skills

The Mathematical Practice Standards are closely aligned with key 21st century student outcomes (Partnership for 21st Century Skills, n.d.; see Table 1.1). Some of these standards include creativity and innovation, critical thinking and problem solving, and communication and collaboration.

Creativity and innovation. Students are encouraged to think creatively using a wide range of ideas, creating new and worth-

Table 1.1

Comparison Across Standards

Standards for Mathematical Practice	21st Century Skills	NAGC Pre-K–Grade 12 Programming Standards
Students make sense of problems and persevere in solving them. Students solve problems in novel ways and pose new mathematical questions of interest to investigate.	Creativity and innovation.	Educators use creative-thinking strategies (Standard 3.4.2). Educators use inquiry models (Standards 3.4.4).
Students reason abstractly and quantitatively. Students attend to precision. Students look for and make use of structure. Students look for and express regularity.	Critical thinking and problem solving.	Educators use critical-thinking strategies (Standard 3.4.1). Educators use problem-solving model strategies (Standard 3.4.3).
Students construct viable arguments and critique the reasoning of others. Students use appropriate tools strategically.	Communication.	Students develop competence in interpersonal and technical communication skills (Standard 4.5).
Students construct viable arguments and critique the reasoning of others.	Collaboration.	Students possess skills in communicating, teaming, and collaborating with diverse individuals and across diverse groups (Standard 4.4).

while ideas, and elaborating and refining their own ideas. They are also expected to work creatively with others by communicating new ideas effectively, being responsive to diverse perspectives, and viewing failure as an opportunity to learn. Moreover, in implementing innovations, students need to learn how to act on creative ideas and make a useful contribution to their field (Partnership for 21st Century Skills, n.d.).

Critical thinking and problem solving. In using these two processes, students need to learn how to reason effectively, use systems thinking to analyze how parts of a whole interact with one another, make judgments and decisions, and solve problems by identifying and asking significant questions that lead to better solutions (Partnership for 21st Century Skills, n.d.).

Communication and collaboration. Students are expected to communicate clearly by articulating their thoughts, listening effectively, using communication for a range of purposes, using and evaluating multiple media and technologies, and communicating effectively in diverse environments. Moreover, they need to learn how to collaborate with others by demonstrating their ability to work effectively and respectfully with diverse teams, exercising flexibility and willingness to be helpful to accomplish a common goal, assuming shared responsibility for collaborative work, and valuing individual contributions (Partnership for 21st Century Skills, n.d.).

Gifted Education Programming Standards

The NAGC Gifted Education Programming Standards (NAGC, 2010) are aligned to the standards of mathematical practice and the 21st century skills (see Table 1.1). For example, gifted and talented students are expected to develop competence in interpersonal and technical communication skills (NAGC, 2010) similar to the 21st century skill of communicating with others and evaluating multiple media. Moreover, teachers of gifted and talented students should use the evidence-based practices of critical thinking, creative thinking, problem solving, and inquiry to encourage students to become independent investigators (NAGC, 2010). Therefore, as educators address one set of national standards, they are addressing others.

Differentiating the Standards

Although the CCSSM standards are strong, they were not developed with the mathematically advanced learner as the focus; therefore, they are not sufficiently advanced to accommodate the needs of most learners who are gifted in mathematics (Johnsen & Sheffield, 2013; VanTassel-Baska, 2013). The CCSSM developers noted that some students may traverse the standards before the end of high school (NGA & CCSSO, 2010b), which will require educators to provide advanced content for them. In addition to subject-based acceleration, educators will also need to enrich the standards by providing more depth, complexity, challenge, and creativity. Educators therefore need a thorough understanding of not only the standards but also the characteristics of gifted and advanced students to differentiate the standards effectively.

Using the CCSSM as a point of departure, we have included differentiation strategies within each of the learning experiences. Educators who teach gifted and advanced students in mathematics might want to use these and other strategies to differentiate the standards (Johnsen & Sheffield, 2013; VanTassel-Baska, 2013).

Acceleration and pacing. Standards and clusters of standards may be identified across grade levels and then compressed within rich problems for more accelerated pacing. Preassessments, curriculum compacting, or above-level testing might be used to determine which students are ready for above-level content (Assouline & Lupkowski-Shoplik, 2011; Colangelo, Assouline, & Gross, 2004). For example, fifth-grade students might be given a problem, such as preparing for the state math assessment, and be required to identify quantitative variables that might improve math performance. Students then might have opportunities to present their data using a variety of graphs; use whole numbers, fractions, or decimals to represent the data; interpret the data using statistical vocabulary; and predict possible trends in student performance. For this book, we decided to select domains that build on one another so that educators can see how to integrate above-level concepts in learning experiences.

Complexity. Complexity can be achieved by solving multistep, abstract problems at an earlier stage of development or by adding more perspectives or connections (Saul, Assouline, & Sheffield, 2010). For example, in the learning experiences presented in Chapter 4, gifted and advanced third-grade students who are studying the growth of plants might consider multiple variables, such as the amount of pebbles, water, soil, and sunlight instead of measuring only the height of the plant.

Creativity. To enhance creativity and innovation, the teacher might want to develop open-ended problems that offer gifted and advanced learners opportunities to pose their own questions (Sheffield, 2006). These questions may be used to assess not only the number of problems posed but also the complexity of the problems—indices of successful problem solvers (Silver & Cai, 1996). In the learning experiences presented in Chapter 4, problem posing is used at the high school level where students might use census at school data to develop research questions they might want to answer; or, at a kindergarten level, students might sort pictures and/or symbols to compare and contrast their groups using mathematical vocabulary. The point is that educators should be open to removing any grade-level-imposed ceilings on the learner's opportunities to explore topics.

Depth. In adding depth, the teacher might ask the student for specialized mathematics vocabulary, details, patterns and trends, or rules (Kaplan, 2009). For example, in the learning experiences presented in Chapter 4, gifted and advanced students in mathematics predict their performance on a physical fitness test, collect data, and then check to see if their prediction was confirmed. They might use mathematical vocabulary to describe not only their performance but also the performance of their classmates. Adding this depth accelerates and enriches the learning experience.

Interdisciplinary connections. Because mathematics is a tool subject, it lends itself for interdisciplinary studies (Kaplan, 2009; VanTassel-Baska, 2004). Many examples are available using interdisciplinary research projects in the learning experiences: comparing and contrasting distances and creating a scale map (social studies and math); examining and predicting which variables might influence animal and plant growth (science and math); analyzing data from a physical fitness test (physical education and math); creating a survey to collect information about classmates' interests, interpreting the results, and planning meaningful activities (language arts, social studies, and math); and using a mark-recapture experiment (science, math, and engineering).

Themes or concepts. Teachers might have students examine the major concepts or themes within and across domains (VanTassel-Baska, 2004). For example, in the set of experiences presented in Chapter 4, the teacher might ask: What are basic principles in mathematics that are important in studying measurement and data? How might these principles apply to statistics and probability or to another domain, such as number and operations? How might the theme of "change" be represented using different languages (e.g., mathematics versus English, English versus art)?

Higher order thinking. Teachers might use deliberate questioning techniques to elevate thinking. For example, using Sheffield's heuristic for innovative and creative mathematicians (Sheffield, 2003; Johnsen & Sheffield, 2013), teachers might ask these questions related to problem solving:

- Relate: How is this problem similar to other mathematical ideas that you have seen? How is it different?
- Investigate: What questions might you ask about this problem?
- Evaluate: Did you answer the question? Does the answer make sense?
- Communicate: What is the best way to let others know what you have discovered?
- Create: What else would you like to find out about this topic?

World applications. Because we live in a global society, it is important for students to see how math is used in posing questions and solving problems that are of concern to the world's citizens (Partnership for 21st Century Skills, n.d.). Many of the problems have quantitative aspects, such as the economy, population growth, obesity, and global warming so that students are able to see the practical applications to their solutions. Results from these studies might be shared with audiences who are interested in making a difference in the world community.

Student interest. To engage students in outcomes that are meaningful to them, teachers might want to provide choices in terms of research projects, problems that might be addressed, ways of learning the mathematics concepts, and products or performances that represent their data. Solving interesting problems nurtures the student's enjoyment, passions, and talent, and often leads to significantly higher achievement gains (Gavin, Casa, Adelson, Carroll, & Sheffield, 2009).

Extracurricular activities. Extracurricular activities such as math clubs, competitions, mentors, online games and courses, Saturday and summer programs, and other experiences should be readily available to students who are gifted and advanced in mathematics. This involvement provides challenge, stimulates interests, and offers opportunities to interact with others of similar abilities (Barbeau & Taylor, 2009).

All of these strategies contribute to the effective differentiation of the standards. Above all, educators need to adjust the instructional pace because advanced learners frequently demonstrate rapid or early mastery of some of the mathematics standards. At the same time, students who are gifted and advanced in mathematics need to delve deeply and creatively into topics, projects, and problems. A combination of both acceleration and enrichment is critical to effective differentiation.

Scope and Sequence

Scopes and sequences are designed to help teachers identify what is expected from their students at a particular grade level and at key points along a learning progression. By studying each learning progression separately and across domains, teachers are able to notice connections and establish learning goals that are above level so that each student is challenged. In this book, we have provided learning progressions within each domain and also showed connections between standards across domains.

Most often, gifted educators use a comprehensive and sequenced core curriculum that is aligned with local, state, and national standards (NAGC, 2010). They then differentiate and expand it to develop differentiated learning plans for Pre-K–12 students (NAGC, 2010). Because of individual variations in experiences, abilities, and responsiveness to different learning experiences, no scope and sequence or learning progression is appropriate for every student. Therefore, educators need to attend to the learning rate and achievement level of each and every student.

The CCSSM have identified domains, standards, and clusters of standards for each grade level and across grade levels. Domains in earlier grades build a foundation for domains in later grades. For example, the Statistics and Probability domain is based on the concepts that were learned within the Measurement and Data domain (To view all of the learning progressions for the CCSSM, see Table 2.1 on page 19.). Teachers need to know about the scope and sequence within a domain and across domains so that major concepts and skills can be introduced, practiced, and extended. For the most part, these learning progressions are based on state and international comparisons, not necessarily on research (NGA & CCSSO, 2010a), so teachers need to be diligent in observing how students respond to curriculum and instruction and pace accordingly. They also need to understand how the domains relate to one another in order to design rich learning experiences that deepen the student's understanding of concepts and principles.

Appendix A in the Common Core State Standards for Mathematics describes four different pathways at the high school level: a traditional pathway, a compacted traditional pathway, an integrated pathway, and a compacted integrated pathway (NGA & CCSSO, 2010b). These accelerated pathways allow advanced students to reach calculus and other college-level courses by their junior or senior years, which is important in preparing them for STEM fields in college (Assouline & Lupkowski-Shoplik, 2011; Colangelo et al., 2004; College Board, 2009). Along with these accelerated courses, students also need to continue developing their passion for mathematics by participating in advanced courses, math clubs, and scientific research so they will pursue STEM fields when they graduate (Bressoud, 2009; Johnsen & Sheffield, 2013; Saul et al., 2010; Wyatt & Wiley, 2010).

Assessments

The chapter on assessments covers the range of assessment activities and measures and spans topics such as types of tests and the implications for decisions. Starting with a discussion of the role of informal assessments in addressing the learner's needs, especially within the context of monitoring the learner's progress with the LEs, the chapter concludes with a discussion of 21st century, computer-based tests that are designed with the Core Curriculum Standards in mind. This chapter also includes a table of standardized tests of mathematical aptitude and achievement that can serve as a resource for teachers. Finally, in keeping with the observation that mathematically talented learners are ready for more complex content at a faster pace, the chapter includes a discussion of above-level testing as a way to determine which students are ready for more accelerated work.

Differentiated Learning Experiences

We have provided prototypical learning experiences that use the Standards for Mathematical Practice—including the one that relates to developing innovative and creative mathematicians—and that support the implementation of the CCSSM. The learning experiences provide examples within two domains and one learning progression (i.e., the Measurement and Data and Statistics and Probability domains). We decided to use one learning progression so that educators might use the examples in developing a scope and sequence of learning experiences within other domains.

Each of the learning experience examples includes these five components:

1. Common Core State Standards are identified for each grade level from kindergarten through high school. In this way, the teacher is able to see both the scope and the sequence within one learning progression.

2. A brief description of the learning experience is provided for both typical and advanced students. This overview compares and contrasts the learning experience for individuals and different groups of students.

3. A sequence of activities is outlined for each learning experience. Activities that are different for the advanced students are *italicized* for easy reference.

4. Implementation strategies are also included at the end of each learning experience. These strategies may include preassessments, grouping, independent research, use of national databases, interdisciplinary problems, and other ways of accelerating and enriching the learning experience.

5. Each learning experience includes suggestions for preassessment and ongoing assessments. For the most part, these assessments provide questions and specific characteristics that might be used in the design of product and performance rubrics or other types of summative assessments.

Management of Differentiated Services

To provide guidance to the teacher in implementing differentiated learning experiences, we have provided specific, concrete examples of ways to manage curriculum and instruction within a single classroom. We have also made suggestions for developing program services and supports within the school and the school district.

Within the classroom, the teacher needs to know how to manage a variety of activities to allow for acceleration and enrichment of gifted and advanced students in mathematics. The teacher needs to establish a system in which students know what they are learning, what resources are available and how to use them, how to demonstrate what they have learned, and what to do next.

Those educators who implement successful systems pay attention to room arrangement, materials management, teacher and student schedules, and teacher and student records. These components work together so that teachers can provide opportunities such as large-group instruction, small-group discussion, paired learning, and individual research activities. They also allow for pacing the curriculum so that it can be more responsive to the individual needs of students.

In developing program services and supports within the school and school district, we have suggested a variety of practical and affordable options: cross-grade-level teaming, moving students across grade levels, classroom schedule changes, or using resources outside of the school. For example, as acceleration for a student occurs within one classroom, subsequent teachers and secondary schools need to accommodate the student as he progresses. Different benchmarks might need to be established for this student, as well as different courses or learning activities. Flexibility is important to ensure that a student continues to be challenged and learns new concepts. This flexibility may require policies to be developed for whole-grade acceleration, content acceleration, grade telescoping, and early entrance options (*Note:* For an extensive discussion of acceleration policy, see Institute for Research and Policy on Acceleration [IRPA], NAGC, & Council of State Directors of Programs for the Gifted [CSDPG], 2009.). Students may also need transportation to enroll in more advanced math courses at the high school, a local community college, or university.

The management of differentiated services therefore requires professional development and collaboration among teachers and administrators within a school, across schools, and within the entire school district. This systemic approach will enable each student to receive the type of instruction needed based on his or her readiness for advanced mathematical concepts.

Resources

We have provided resources in the appendices that include a glossary, an annotated bibliography of critical readings, and suggested teacher resources. Each of these materials has evidence of its effectiveness with gifted and advanced learners in mathematics. We have included key words in the glossary in Appendix A. Appendix B provides an annotated bibliography of critical readings in mathematics education. The readings range from books and journal articles about mathematics and gifted education to reports written by national organizations about the current state of mathematics education in the United States. Appendix C provides a list of annotated resources for teachers in using the CCSSM or in differentiating instruction in mathematics. For example, the University of Arizona has developed learning progressions of mathematical topics across grade levels (e.g., K–6 geometry) and the National Council of Teachers of Mathematics has created an online resource called Real World Math.

Conclusion

The CCSSM standards are strong, but they were not developed with the gifted and advanced learner as the focus. The importance of differentiating the CCSSM is essential not only to develop the knowledge and skills of learners who are mathematically talented but to also develop their passion for math. In this chapter, we provided an overview of how different standards relate to one another and are integrated within gifted education practices, particularly in the areas of interpersonal and technical communication skills and thinking processes, such as critical and creative thinking, problem solving, and inquiry. We also included an overview of strategies for differentiating the CCSSM, which included acceleration and pacing, creativity, depth, and complexity, among others. We suggested that knowledge of the scope and sequence's organization within the CCSSM can enhance the gifted education teacher's comprehension of connections across grade levels in providing for acceleration and across mathematics domains in developing the student's depth of understanding. Furthermore, we emphasized the use of different types of assessments in determining gifted and advanced students' readiness for differentiated learning experiences. Differentiation would not be possible without the teachers' knowledge of how to manage a variety of activities that allow for both acceleration and enrichment. In the following chapters, we will describe in more detail how the scope and sequence in mathematics is organized into learning progressions and ways that educators might not only use assessments in differentiating their lessons but also how to implement differentiation within the classroom, school, and district.

Chapter 2

Adapting Learning Progressions for Gifted and Advanced Learners

Because learning is an ongoing developmental progression and takes place over time, a *learning progression*, or a more traditional *scope and sequence*, is designed to help teachers identify what is expected from their students and the key points along a path that indicate growth in a student's knowledge and skills. Teachers' knowledge of learning progressions is important in their understanding of the articulation of essential core concepts and processes in each domain within and across grade levels so that their students develop a deeper, broader, and more sophisticated understanding of the "big ideas" of mathematics (Hess, 2008). By examining each progression separately and across domains, teachers are able to identify how standards change and increase in rigor for the student, to see how they are connected to one another, and to establish learning goals so that each student is challenged and experiences continuous progress from elementary to middle to high school and to higher education and professional careers. Progressions are also useful in designing formative and summative assessments and ensuring that above-level standards are included so that gifted and advanced students' strengths in knowledge and skills can be identified.

In mathematics education, these progressions also may be labeled *learning trajectories* if they define key interventions (Consortium for Policy Research in Education [CPRE], 2011). The difference between learning trajectories and learning progressions is that the trajectories are based not only on the logic of mathematics but also on how a student's thinking grows *in response to learning experiences* (Sarama & Clements, 2009). The trajectories, therefore, are able to provide an empirical basis for choices about when to teach what to whom (CPRE, 2011). When gifted and advanced learners are engaged in problem-based learning that deepens their understanding of complex concepts, their growth may accelerate their trajectory and they may be ready for even more rigorous mathematical challenges (Teague et al., 2011).

Because of these individual variations in experiences, abilities, and responsiveness to different educational interventions, no universal trajectories or progressions exist that are appropriate for every student. For students who are gifted and advanced in mathematics, they may proceed through learning progressions in a different sequence and at a different pace than their peers. For example, mapping backward from a set of desired outcomes (such as college) to create a learning progression may be too steep for some students, yet not steep enough for others. Teachers need to be aware of the learning progressions for a typical learner and ways of adapting them for gifted and advanced learners. As the authors of the CCSSM state, "No set of grade-specific standards can fully reflect the great variety in abilities, needs, learning rates, and achievement levels of students in any given classroom" (NGA & CCSSO, 2010a, p. 4). This chapter will describe the CCSSM learning progressions within and across domains and ways that they might be adapted for gifted and advanced learners.

Table 2.1

Learning Progressions Within Mathematical Domains

K	1	2	3	4	5	6	7	8	High School
Counting and Cardinality									Number and Quantity
Number and Operations in Base Ten						Ratios and Proportional Relationships			
			Number and Operations—Fractions			The Number System			
Operations and Algebraic Thinking						Expressions and Equations			Algebra
									Functions / Modeling / Functions
Geometry						Geometry			Geometry
Measurement and Data						Statistics and Probability			Statistics and Probability

Description of Learning Progressions

The CCSSM describe domains within each band of grades. As can be seen in Table 2.1, domains in earlier grades build a foundation for domains in later grades.

For example, the Counting and Cardinality domain and the Operations and Algebraic Thinking domain are related to understanding and using numbers. This strand begins with early counting, which in turn leads to the basic operations of addition, subtraction, multiplication, and division. Students next build their understanding of the properties of arithmetic and use their understanding to solve real-world and mathematical problems. Next, they extend operations into the system of rational numbers. As the students understand the meaning and properties of operations, they concurrently develop computational methods (e.g., single-digit to multidigit) with whole and fractional numbers. The study of ratios and proportional relationships at the middle school level extends the students' earlier studies in measurement and in multiplication and division. Students will eventually use these ratios in geometry, algebra, and calculus (Institute for Mathematics and Education, 2012).

As can be seen, the domains within each of the strands form the foundation for not only that strand but also many of the other mathematical strands. Teachers therefore need to know about the progressions within a domain or strand and across domains so that major concepts and skills can be introduced, practiced, and extended.

Within Domains

The Institute for Mathematics and Education (IME, 2012) at the University of Arizona has identified progressions within each of these domains based on the logical structure of mathematics and research on children's cognitive development. For example, within the Measurement and Data domain (grades K–5), students work with data, which provides the foundation for the Statistics and Probability domain (grades 6–high school). Kindergarten students count and compare objects, first and second graders solve addition and subtraction problems using data, and third through fifth graders solve problems using the number line and fractional concepts using the four operations. At these grade levels, one progression dealing with categorical data, which focuses on sorting objects and bar graphs, eventually leads to bivariate categorical data and two-way tables by the eighth grade. The other progression dealing with measurement data, which focuses on students' development of different types of graphs and line plots to represent specific units of measurement, leads to the students' understanding of statistical variability, chance processes and probability models, correlations, and an expanded array of functions at the middle and high school levels. Context is emphasized throughout so that students will understand that data are more than numbers; they are used to answer questions about events and to pose other questions.

Each of the domains is further divided into standards and clusters of standards for each grade level. The standards define what students should understand and be able to do and the clusters are groups of related standards. In continuing with our example of the Measurement and Data domain, a cluster sequence for Grades K–5 is listed in Table 2.2.

In examining the clusters of standards, it is easy to see how one cluster builds on the next one. For example, students would need to understand how to measure length in standard units (see Grade 2 in Table 2.2) before recognizing perimeter versus area measurements (see Grade 3 in Table 2.2). Beginning in the first grade, students start learning about ways of representing and interpreting data that continues through the fifth grade. Note that the number of clusters within each of the grade levels varies so that at the kindergarten level, there are only two clusters of standards, whereas at the second- and third-grade levels, there are four clusters of standards in the Measurement and Data domain.

The standards further distinguish the characteristics of the clusters for each level. For example, "Represent and Interpret

Table 2.2
Sequence of Clusters Within the Measurement of Data Domain

Kindergarten	Grade 1	Grade 2	Grade 3	Grade 4	Grade 5
Describe and compare measurable attributes.	Measure lengths indirectly and by iterating length units.	Measure and estimate lengths in standard units.	Solve problems involving measurement and estimation of intervals of time, liquid volumes, and masses of objects.	Solve problems involving measurement and conversion of measurements from a larger unit to a smaller unit.	Convert like measurement units within a given measurement system.
Classify objects and count the number of objects in categories.	Tell and write time.	Relate addition and subtraction to length.	Represent and interpret data.	Represent and interpret data.	Represent and interpret data.
	Represent and interpret data.	Work with time and money.	Geometric measurement: Understand concepts of area and relate area to multiplication and addition.	Geometric measurement: Understand concepts of angle and measure angles.	Geometric measurement: Understand concepts of volume and relate volume to multiplication and to addition.
		Represent and interpret data.	Geometric measurement: Recognize perimeter as an attribute of plan figures and distinguish between linear and area measures.		

Data," which is a cluster heading across grades 1–5, is delineated within the standards in Table 2.3.

The standards provide clarity in identifying (a) the ways that students represent data through line plots, picture graphs, and bar graphs; (b) how their measurements become more precise as they measure to the nearest fraction; and (c) how the problems they are solving become more complex. Examining the standards in this way enables teachers to assess students' knowledge and skills above and below grade level and accelerate gifted and advanced students as needed. For example, a student already may be able to solve problems using data presented in picture graphs and bar graphs and be ready to solve problems using data from line plots. (*Note:* See the learning experiences in the Sample Activities on pp. 52–91 for examples of differentiation of the clusters and related standards.) Again, note the variation in the number of standards related to the cluster "Represent and Interpret Data." More standards are introduced within this domain at the second- and third-grade levels than at other grade levels.

As mentioned in the CCSSM documents, "What students can learn at any particular grade level depends upon what they have learned before" (NGA & CCSSO, 2010a, p. 5). Moreover, the authors of the standards cautioned that the learning progressions are based on state and international comparisons, not necessarily on research. Therefore, it is important that teachers identify clusters and related standards that meet the needs of individual students based on their previous knowledge and performance and their responsiveness to the curriculum and instruction.

Across Domains

In addition to the sequences of standards and the relationships across standard clusters within a domain, standards are also related to each other across domains. Again, as an example, the Measurement and Data domain not only builds a foundation for the Statistics and Probability domain but is also related to other domains (see Table 2.4). For instance, within the Numbers

Table 2.3

Standards for the Cluster Heading "Represent and Interpret Data"

Grade 1	Grade 2	Grade 3	Grade 4	Grade 5
Organize, represent, and interpret data with up to three categories; ask and answer questions about the total number of data points, how many are in each category, and how many more/less are in one category than in another.	Generate measurement data by measuring lengths of several objects to the nearest whole unit, or by making the repeated measurements of the same object. Show the measurements by making a line plot, where the horizontal scale is marked off in whole-number units.	Draw a scaled picture graph to represent a data set with several categories. Solve one- and two-step "how many more" and "how many less" problems using information presented in scaled bar graphs.	Make a line plot to display a data set of measurements in fractions of a unit (1/2, 1/4, 1/8). Solve problems involving addition and subtraction of fractions by using information presented in line plots.	Make a line plot to display a data set of measurements in fractions of a unit (1/2, 1/4, 1/8). Use operations on fractions for this grade to solve problems involving information presented in line plots.
	Draw a picture graph and a bar graph (with single-unit scale) to represent a data set with up to four categories. Solve simple put-together, take-apart, and compare problems using the information presented in a bar graph.	Generate measurement data by measuring lengths using rulers marked with halves and fourths of an inch. Show the data by making a line plot, where the horizontal scale is marked off in appropriate units—whole numbers, halves, or quarters.		

Table 2.4

Relationships Across Mathematical Domains for Measurement and Data for Grade 3

Number and Operations	Operations and Algebraic Thinking	Geometry	Measurement and Data
3.NF: Represent a fraction 1/*b* on a number line diagram by defining the interval from 0 to 1 as the whole and partitioning it into *b* equal parts.	3.OA: Use multiplication and division to solve word problems in situations involving measurement quantities.	3.G: Partition shapes into parts with equal areas.	3.MD: Solve problems involving measurement and estimation of intervals, of time, liquid, volume, and masses of objects.

and Operations: Fractions domain for grade 3, students need to know how a number line can be divided into equal units using *measurement* and how fractions are parts with equal *measurements*. In the Geometry domain, shapes are partitioned into parts with equal areas and *measuring* length allows students to understand formulas that are used to find area and volume. In the Operations and Algebraic Thinking domain, students must use operations to solve word problems in situations involving *measurement* quantities.

Athough only one grade is illustrated in Table 2.4, each of the grades and bands of grades has similar connections across domains. The understanding of how the domains relate to one another is essential in building the breadth and depth needed for designing rich learning experiences for gifted and advanced students. Again, the standards can be differentiated within each of the domains by accelerating and combining student outcomes and across the domain by adding more complexity to the problems being solved.

In summary, domains, which are divided into grade level standards and clusters of standards, build upon and are linked to one another. Cross-grade-level clusters of standards provide greater clarity for incorporating more depth and complexity in problems and in ways of compacting the standards for gifted and advanced students. Teachers, therefore, need to become familiar with the standards at their own level and also across levels so that they know when to extend and accelerate each student's knowledge and skills.

Standards for Mathematical Practice

The Standards for Mathematical Practice "describe varieties of expertise that mathematics educators at all levels should develop in their students" (NGA & CCSSO, 2010a, pp. 6–8). These standards should be integrated into learning experiences throughout the different domains and at all levels to encourage students' investigations of a variety of problems (see Standards for Mathematical Practice in Chapter 1).

In supporting mathematically advanced students to persevere, be more creative, and to take risks in the face of failure, Johnsen and Sheffield (2013) proposed a ninth standard: "Solve problems in novel ways and pose new mathematical questions of interest to investigate" (p. 16). With this new practice standard, students would be encouraged to embrace challenge and become math innovators.

Continuing with the example from the Measurement and Data domain, the Standards of Mathematical Practice might be developed in gifted and advanced students through the inclusion of this four-step investigative process:

- Pose questions that can be answered with data.
- Design and use a research plan to collect relevant data.
- Analyze the data with appropriate methods.
- Interpret results and draw valid conclusions from the data that relate to the question.

Learning progressions in the CCSSM describe the knowledge and skills (i.e., the "what") and the grade bands (i.e., the "when"). It is equally important for educators to remember to integrate the Standards of Mathematical Practice within each of their classroom learning experiences (i.e., the "how"). In this way, teachers pay attention not only to a carefully crafted and sequenced set of standards that meet each student's needs but also encourage students to investigate rich mathematical concepts in depth, applying innovative mathematical reasoning to a variety of problems.

Sequence of Courses at the Middle School and High School Level

Appendix A in the *Common Core State Standards for Mathematics* describes four pathways at the high school level: a traditional pathway, a compacted traditional pathway, an integrated pathway, and a compacted integrated pathway (NGA & CCSSO, 2010b). The traditional pathway consists of two algebra courses and a geometry course. The compacted version of the traditional pathway, where no content is omitted, is where students complete the content of the seventh- and eighth-grade courses in the seventh grade, and the high school algebra course (Algebra I) in the eighth grade. This accelerated trajectory allows advanced students to reach calculus or other college-level courses by their junior or senior year.

The integrated pathway consists of a sequence of three courses, with each including number and quantity, algebra, functions, geometry, statistics, and probability. The compacted version of the integrated pathway is similar to the compacted version of the traditional pathway. The seventh- and eighth-grade math courses are combined into a single compacted course in the seventh grade. At the eighth-grade level, the students take the high school Mathematics I course (*Note:* See Appendix A of the CCSSM for an overview of each pathway organized by course, conceptual category, clusters, and standards.). Each of these courses should integrate the Standards for Mathematical Practice so that they are challenging and relevant to the students.

Students who take advanced courses in high school, such as precalculus and calculus, are better prepared for STEM fields and tend to do better in college than those who do not (Adelman, 1999; Colangelo et al., 2004; College Board, 2009; Kolitch & Brody, 1992). Along with acceleration, it is important that gifted and advanced students continue to develop their passion for mathematics by pursuing advanced coursework in high school or college such as statistics, mathematical decision making, and discrete mathematics and/or by participating in extracurricular activities such as apprenticeships, math clubs, scientific research, and competitions so that they will enjoy math and pursue STEM fields when they graduate (Bressoud, 2009; Johnsen & Sheffield, 2013; Wyatt & Wiley, 2010).

Differentiating the Learning Progressions

The learning progressions in the CCSSM provide a framework or a general map for learning but should not be construed as a single route to a destination (Hess & Kearns, 2011). This flexibility allows for many opportunities for differentiation. Some of these strategies include:

- *Providing appropriate pacing and acceleration.* By studying the standards and the clusters of standards, teachers can identify concepts that are above level. Including these above level concepts on pre- and ongoing assessments raises the ceiling and allows the teacher to identify what students know. Teachers can then integrate new, challenging concepts into class problems or compact the curriculum, allowing students to do alternative problems that match their current level of achievement. For example, some students might be using bar graphs to represent data while others might be using line plot graphs or designing their own experiments using their math knowledge instead of collecting data for previously designed experiments. In some cases, when students are learning concepts that are two or more grade levels beyond the typical learner, the principal and other decision makers may want to consider other acceleration options such as single-subject acceleration, grade skipping, or early entrance into secondary or special schools (*Note:* See Colangelo et al., 2004, for a cogent discussion of types of acceleration.).

- *Integrating greater complexity and depth in problems.* Teachers can develop complex problems by including abstract concepts, steps that involve one or more operations, novel situations, and/or information that is not relevant to solving the problem (Chamberlin, 2010). They might also use advanced mathematical vocabulary, ask students to compare and contrast different problem-solving methods, look for trends and patterns, pose new questions, or identify a new mathematical rule (Kaplan, 2009).

- *Focusing on broader concepts.* Teachers might develop units around broader mathematical concepts or themes. For example, students might examine the concept of "order" by (a) identifying situations in which the order in data communicates a concept, (b) collecting examples of situations in which ordered data have allowed for predictions, (c) establishing criteria to distinguish between examples of natural and constructed order, and/or (d) by speculating on ways in which random occurrences might be used to form new concepts of order.

- *Incorporating more creativity in problem solving.* Sheffield (2000) identified the criteria for assessment to encourage students to become creative and investigative mathematicians: depth of understanding, fluency, flexibility, originality, elaboration or elegance, generalizations, and extensions. For example, the teacher might develop more ambiguous problems for which the student needs to create an algorithm instead of using a familiar one. Students might provide different correct answers, methods or solutions (fluency), different categories of methods or solutions (flexibility), solutions that show insight (originality), or clarity and quality of expression (elaboration). Students might also use multiple ways of representing data, posing their own questions, creating their own experiments, and creating data-gathering instruments that address the questions.

- *Asking higher level thinking questions.* Questions should encourage students to make comparisons, predictions, and draw conclusions about the problems that they are identifying or solving. For example, using the data, what might you predict about the student's performance? Were your predictions correct? Draw conclusions about the student's performance and describe the trend. What factors might have influenced the student's performance? Moreover, students should have opportunities to reflect on ways that they solved problems and on their own reasoning—metacognitive thinking. How did you arrive at your solution? Are there other ways you might have solved the problem?

- *Using the same processes mathematicians might use.* Students need to have opportunities to work through problems in the same ways that a mathematician might. Problems need to be ambiguous and multifaceted, requiring students to think deeply about both the process and possible solutions. For example, the teacher might present more complex problems to gifted and advanced students in math as a challenge (not for a grade or course credit) to try and solve over longer periods of time.

- *Creating authentic, interdisciplinary problem-solving opportunities.* Because math is a tool subject, it lends itself to solving problems that include many other disciplines. For example, in the social sciences, students might estimate the population of their school, the city, the state, the U.S., and other countries to predict future population growth. In the health field, students might design experiments to compare body weight and eating habits. The interdisciplinary connections are endless and can address issues that are important to gifted and advanced students. Interdisciplinary thinking may also be promoted by having students operationally define purposefully ambiguous terms (Lesh, Hoover, Hole, Kelly, & Post, 2000). For example, many model eliciting activities (MEAs), such as "on-time arrival," have engaged students in precollege thinking.

- *Grouping students with similar interests and abilities.* Using formative assessments, teachers can identify those students who are ready for above-level content and homogeneously group these students together. Students might also be grouped around areas of interest. For example, several students might want to design a study to examine the inclusion of girls in different high school sports and the resources needed to support both girls' and boys' competitions. Researchers have reported that full-time ability grouping produces substantial academic gains for gifted students and encourages critical thinking and creativity (Kulik, 2004; Kulik & Kulik, 1982, 1984; Rogers, 1991, 2007; Vaughn, 1990).

- *Identifying collaborators.* Mathematicians in higher education or within the community provide not only expert instruction and opportunities to work with authentic, complex problems but also provide an introduction to professional networks and the work habits that are required in a professional field. Many of the models in gifted education lend themselves to the involvement of collaborators and mentors such as Renzulli's Enrichment Triad Model (Renzulli, 1977), Purdue's Three Stage Model (Feldhusen & Kolloff, 1986), the Autonomous Learner Model (Betts & Kercher, 1999), and the SMPY Model (Assouline & Lupkowski-Shoplik, 2011; Lupkowski, Assouline, & Stanley, 1990). In each of these models, mentors are involved in stimulating the student's interests and involving her deeply in the methods of the discipline. For educators in small communities, collaborators, and mentors might also be accessed using distance learning and might include other educators as well as students.

- *Engaging students in outside-of-school opportunities.* Afterschool or summer programs provide students with opportunities to work in an authentic context, such as in a laboratory, on a team with other researchers, and/ or with mathematicians at the university level. Middle school and secondary students might also be interested in university or fast-paced high school courses. Talent search programs are available to identify, assess, and recognize students with exceptional talent in mathematics (see Appendix C). They also provide students with opportunities to interact with like peers in a stimulating environment. Students might also compete in state and national competitions such as the Intel Science Talent Search or Mathcounts, enabling them to interact with other students who have talents in mathematics and other STEM fields (Rusczyk, 2010).

Getting Started in Differentiating the Learning Progressions

In getting started, curriculum directors and teachers in role-alike groups (e.g., K–2 teachers, 3–5 teachers) should examine the standards at their band of grade levels. This process will allow teachers to identify learning progressions and the important concepts, processes, and student outcomes within and across domains.

Once this initial work is completed, teachers across all grades will want to meet to compare learning progressions to ensure a comprehensive and coherent structure across all of the grades. At this time, acceleration options need to be discussed. These might include the different secondary options, as well as ways to advance students through a learning progression as they demonstrate mastery of foundational concepts. Teachers will need to consider students who are achieving above grade level. How will subsequent teachers provide for these gifted and advanced students? How will the curriculum be adapted? Will there be administrative options, such as single subject acceleration, grade skipping, or early entrance to high school or college?

After this work is completed, the teachers will want to examine the curriculum and the units that they have already developed, review student work samples, and identify how these relate to the standards' learning progressions. This process will uncover whether or not the curricular units build the students' understanding of key concepts over time. Teachers will also want to look at ways that they can adapt or differentiate the units for gifted learners (see pp. 52–91 for sample differentiated learning experiences for typical and advanced learners).

Once the curricular units are designed and differentiated, teacher teams will want to identify available human and material resources. At this point, they may even want to consider developing partnerships with universities, identifying competitions, and involving students in distance learning opportunities for extensions.

The final step in this process is to "test" the validity of the learning progression and its effects on all of the students. In validating and refining the progressions and identifying students' learning trajectories, the teacher will want to use and develop formative, ongoing, and summative types of assessments, which is the topic of our next chapter.

Conclusion

Learning progressions or more traditional scopes and sequences help teachers identify what is expected from students and key benchmarks within and across grade levels. Knowing how standards are connected to one another, both vertically and horizontally, helps educators establish goals that challenge each learner, build a foundation for subsequent knowledge and skills, and develop above-level assessments. Given the lack of research on learning progressions, teachers need to adapt them not only for gifted and advanced learners but for typical learners as well.

Chapter 3

Assessment

Introduction

Educational assessment is a complex term that encompasses a range of activities and experiences and yields information useful for placement and programming decisions, as well as for monitoring student progress. Educational decisions about the learner can range along a decision-making continuum of informal to formal. Examples of informal assessment include those that are found in the LEs and are discussed in the first part of this chapter. Educators working with gifted and advanced learners within the Common Core State Standards also need to conduct preassessments to determine which experiences are most relevant for the typical as well as the advanced learner. The chapter includes the following:

- informal and formal assessments relevant for implementing the LEs,
- qualitative and quantitative assessments relevant for implementing the LEs,
- traditional assessment of mathematics achievement,
- above-level assessment, and
- 21st century assessments.

Qualitative and Quantitative Assessments Relevant for Implementing Learning Experiences

The CCSSM provide performance expectations for the end of each grade. Using these performance expectations, assessment systems can be implemented to determine mastery of content. These assessment systems include preassessment, ongoing assessment, and summative assessments. As a part of the learning experience, the teacher will implement both preassessment and ongoing assessment procedures, which will vary according to the grade and lesson. These assessment procedures may include both quantitative measures as well as qualitative measures.

In our LE examples in the Sample Activities on pages 52–91, there are varying degrees of formality associated with all aspects of assessment. For example, in the Grade 1 LE, the teacher administers a more formal preassessment to determine the students' knowledge and skills related to interpreting graphs, whereas in the Grade 3 LE, the teacher uses observations and questioning to determine the students' considerations of multiple variables.

Ryser (2011) cogently described three methods of qualitative assessments: interviews, observations, and performance-based assessments. The latter two are most pertinent to this discussion. Observations, in particular, are relevant to the informal assessment described in the Learning Experience examples. Ryser's discussion of a system of jotting down observed behavior is presented within a broader discussion of identification for gifted programming; however, jot-downs also are applicable to the more specific situation of a learning experience As she described, "When teachers observe a student exhibiting this characteristic [offers unusual or unique responses], they jot down the student's name in the box that contains this characteristic" (p. 45).

Product- and performance-based assessments allow for a more quantitative approach for observing the learner's behaviors.

Performance-based assessments include an evaluation component but are typically documented through a predetermined rubric, shown in Figure 3.1. An excellent example of a rubric is found in *Using the Common Core State Standards for Mathematics With Gifted and Advanced Learners* (Johnsen & Sheffield, 2013).

Curriculum-based assessments (CBA), which measure a set of skills from specific curriculum materials, are another quantitative approach to connecting classroom content with the assessment process. This system offers the teacher a baseline against which progress can be measured. Additionally, because CBA are closely linked to the curriculum, instruction is directly linked to the results. This system helps to assure that there are no gaps in the learner's background knowledge and that students who might be struggling have access to appropriate interventions.

Indeed, the needs of *all* students—struggling and advanced—are now front and center for educators, thanks in large part to the coalescing of two separate educational topics: the core curriculum and Response to Intervention (RtI). Although originally designed to provide timely (e.g., early) and tiered interventions for students struggling in reading or math, educators of gifted students quickly realized that the general principles were readily adaptable to the needs of gifted learners with the inclusion of challenging tasks that were above level (Coleman & Johnsen, 2013; Johnsen, Sulak, & Rollins, 2012). Although a comprehensive discussion of RtI is beyond the scope of this book, it is important for readers to know that in the general and special educational communities, there is a strong connection between RtI and the core curriculum, and educators of gifted students recognize the validity of the general concepts of RtI in differentiating the curriculum.

Teachers of gifted students must keep in mind that high-ability students require assessment of their problem-solving and application skills (not just lower order skills as measured through an assessment of mathematical operations, often a main aspect of universal screening and progress monitoring). To be comprehensive, an assessment must take into consideration other

Assessment Criteria	1 Novice	2 Apprentice	3 Proficient	4 Distinguished
Depth of Understanding	Little or no understanding	Partial understanding; minor mathematical errors	Good understanding; mathematically correct	In-depth understanding; well-developed ideas
Fluency	One incomplete or unworkable strategy or technique	At least one appropriate solution with strategy or technique shown	At least two appropriate solutions, may use the same strategy or technique	Several appropriate solutions, may use the same strategy or technique
Flexibility	No method apparent	At least one method (e.g., all graphs, all algebraic equations and so on)	At least two methods of solution (e.g., geometric, graphical, algebraic, physical modeling)	Three or more methods of solution (e.g., geometric, graphical, algebraic, physical modeling)
Originality	Method may be different but does not lead to a solution	Method will lead to a solution but is fairly common	Unusual, workable method used by only a few students, or uncommon solution	Unique, insightful method or solution used only by one or two students
Elaboration or Elegance	Little or no appropriate explanation given	Explanation is understandable, but is unclear in some places	Clear explanation using correct mathematical terms	Clear, concise, precise explanations making good use of graphs, charts, models, or equations
Generalizations and Reasoning	No generalizations made, or they are incorrect and reasoning is unclear	At least one correct generalization made; but not well-supported with clear reasoning	At least one well-made, supported generalization, or more than one correct but unsupported generalization	Several well-supported generalizations; clear reasoning
Extensions	No related mathematical question explored	At least one related mathematical question appropriately explored	One related question explored in-depth, or more than one question appropriately explored	More than one related question explored in-depth

Figure 3.1. Scoring rubric to encourage mathematical creativity. From "Creating and Developing Promising Young Mathematicians" by L. J. Sheffield, 2000, *Teaching Children Mathematics*, *6*, p. 416–419, 426. Copyright 2000 by the National Council of Teachers of Mathematics. Reprinted with permission from the National Council of Teachers of Mathematics.

information about the student's learning environment, such as availability of advanced curriculum as well as psychosocial factors (e.g., level of motivation). For the mathematically able student, CBA and progress monitoring as delineated in RtI models are important complements to informal and standardized measures that comprise a comprehensive approach to assessment. In the following sections, we describe several norm-referenced, quantitative tests that were developed by major testing companies and/or consortia. Table 3.1 provides a summary of assessments.

Traditional Assessment of Mathematics Aptitude

Aptitude tests are designed to measure potential to learn. Some tests were developed specifically to assist the educator with placement and others were designed to be more diagnostic. These are not mutually exclusive concepts and some tests— for example, the Cognitive Abilities Test (CogAT; Lohman, 2011)—can do both. For an extensive discussion of the technical qualities of traditional assessment of mathematical/quantitative reasoning aptitude, see pages 75–118 (Robins & Jolly, 2011) of *Identifying Gifted Students* (Johnsen, 2011) and *Developing Math Talent* (Assouline & Lupkowski-Shoplik, 2011). Assouline and Lupkowski-Shoplik (2011) discussed quantitative aptitude as measured by group-ability tests such as the CogAT and also presented brief descriptions of a variety of different mathematics aptitude tests, including:

1. Iowa Algebra Aptitude Test (IAAT),
2. Orleans-Hanna Algebra Prognosis Test,
3. Test of Early Mathematics Ability—Third Edition,
4. Test of Mathematical Ability—Second Edition, and
5. Test of Mathematical Ability for Gifted Students (TOMAGS).

Table 3.1

Summary of Tests

Test Name (Publisher)	Construct Measured/ Group or Individual	Purpose for Administering	Age or Grade Level of Student	Who Can Administer
Cognitive Abilities Test (CogAT-7) (Riverside Publishing)	Verbal aptitude, quantitative aptitude, nonverbal aptitude/ Group	To measure cognitive ability; may be used for placement in gifted program; includes a gifted screening form	Grades K–12	Certified educator
Comprehensive Testing Program 4 (CTP 4) (Educational Records Bureau)	Achievement/Group (Verbal and quantitative reasoning skills are assessed as well. Can also be administered above level.)	Assessment of school material learned	Grades 1–10	Certified educator
Iowa Assessments (formerly the Iowa Tests of Basic Skills [ITBS]) (Riverside Publishing)	Achievement/Group (When administered above grade level, it measures aptitude)	Assessment of school material learned	Grades K–8	Certified educator
Iowa Algebra Aptitude Test (5th ed., IAAT) (Riverside Publishing)	Specific readiness for learning algebra/Group or individual	Placement into prealgebra or algebra	Grades 7–8 (4–6 as above level)	Certified educator
KeyMath–3 Diagnostic Assessment (Pearson)	Math achievement and aptitude/Individual	Diagnostic, primarily to determine presence of a disability; less useful for obtaining information about programming for math talented students	Ages 5–22	Certified educator

Table 3.1, *continued*

Test Name (Publisher)	Construct Measured/ Group or Individual	Purpose for Administering	Age or Grade Level of Student	Who Can Administer
Measure of Academic Progress (MAP) (Northwest Evaluation Association)	Reading, mathematics, and language usage/Individually administered computer-adaptive test	Assessments in reading, mathematics, and language, which are aligned with state standards	Grades 2–10	Certified educator
Orleans-Hanna Algebra Prognosis Test (3rd ed.) (Pearson)	Specific readiness for learning algebra/Group or individual	Placement into prealgebra or algebra	Grades 7–11 (4–6 as above level)	Certified educator
Otis-Lennon School Ability Test (8th ed., OLSAT) (Pearson)	Verbal and nonverbal aptitude/ Group	To measure cognitive ability; may be used for placement in gifted programs	Grades K–12	Certified educator
School and College Ability Test (SCAT) (Johns Hopkins University Center for Talented Youth)	General measure of scholastic aptitude/Group	Primarily used as an above-level talent search measure	Grades 2–6	Certified educator
Screening Assessment for Gifted Elementary and Middle School Students (SAGES-2) (Prufrock Press)	Nonverbal aptitude; achievement/Group	Primarily used for gifted screening; identifies student's performance in math; gifted norms	Grades K–8	Certified educator
Sequential Tests of Educational Progress (STEP) (Johns Hopkins University Center for Talented Youth)	Broad global achievement/ Individual	Assessment of school material learned; often used above level	Grades K–12	Certified educator

Table 3.1, *continued*

Test Name (Publisher)	Construct Measured/ Group or Individual	Purpose for Administering	Age or Grade Level of Student	Who Can Administer
Slosson Intelligence Test–Revised (3rd ed., SIT–R) (Slosson Educational Publications)	Emphasis on verbal ability/ Individual	Appropriate for screening for gifted program; less useful for programming for math talented students	Ages 4–65	Certified educator or psychologist
Stanford Achievement Test (10th ed., Stanford 10) (Pearson)	General achievement of school subjects/Group	Assessment of school material learned	Grades K–12	Certified educator
Stanford-Binet (Revised Regularly) (Riverside)	General intelligence/Individual	Measure of general ability for placement and programming purposes; especially useful when diagnosing some disabilities	Ages 2–adult	Licensed or certified psychologist
Test of Early Mathematics Ability (3rd ed.) (Pro–Ed)	Achievement in mathematics/ Individual	Assessment of learning problems	Ages 3–8	Certified educator
Test of Mathematical Abilities (2nd ed., TOMA–2) (Pro–Ed)	Achievement in mathematics/ Individual or group	Assessment of learning problems	Ages 8–18	Certified educator
Test of Mathematical Abilities for Gifted Students (TOMAGS) (Pro–Ed)	Math reasoning and problem-solving ability/Individual or group	Screening for math reasoning	Grades K–6	Certified educator

Table 3.1, *continued*

Test Name (Publisher)	Construct Measured/ Group or Individual	Purpose for Administering	Age or Grade Level of Student	Who Can Administer
Wechsler Individual Achievement Tests (3rd ed., WIAT-III) (Psychological Corporation)	Achievement in reading, mathematics, and language/ Individual	Measure of general achievement often for placement and programming purposes; especially useful when diagnosing some disabilities	Grades pre-K–college	Licensed or certified psychologist
Wechsler Intelligence Scales (Psychological Corporation)	General intelligence/Individual	Measure of general ability for placement and programming purposes; especially useful when diagnosing some disabilities	Three versions of the test exist, one for each age level: Preschool/Primary, School, and Adult (each is revised regularly)	Licensed or certified psychologist
Woodcock-Johnson III NU (Tests of Cognitive Abilities and Tests of Achievement) (Riverside)	Achievement in reading, mathematics, and language/ Individual	Measure of general achievement	Ages 2–90+	Licensed or certified psychologist, or specially trained educator (computer scored)
Woodcock-Johnson III NU Tests of Cognitive Abilities (Riverside)	General cognitive ability/ Individual	Measure of general ability for placement and programming purposes	Ages 2–90+	Licensed or certified psychologist, or specially trained educator (computer scored)

From *Developing Math Talent: A Comprehensive Guide to Math Education for Gifted Students in Elementary and Middle School* (2nd ed., pp. 97–100) by S. G. Assouline and A. E. Lupkowski-Shoplik. 2011, Waco, TX: Prufrock Press. Copyright 2011 by Prufrock Press. Adapted with permission.

Traditional Assessment of Mathematics Achievement

Achievement tests were developed to measure what students have learned and are built on the assumption that the test measures what students have learned *recently*. This is a reasonable assumption for the typical student—yet not necessarily for the advanced learner. In fact, advanced learners are often considered advanced because of their very high performance on grade-based achievement tests. Furthermore, demonstrated high performance may be regarded as indicative of mastery of skills measured by the test. Assouline and Lupkowski-Shoplik (2011) suggested that,

> "Familiarity with the major achievement tests that are available in schools will help educators and parents understand the degree of information available through results obtained from the tests. These results can be used to compare a student's progress to others and can serve as a baseline when measuring future progress" (p. 77).

Grade-level achievement tests have been serving schools, teachers, and students for decades and, over the years, they have been revised, renormed, redesigned, and in some cases, renamed. For example, one of the more commonly used tests, the *Iowa Tests of Basic Skills* (ITBS), which started as a test for Iowa students, has been in existence since the mid-1930s. But times have changed and so have the tests. Indeed, in 2012, the ITBS evolved to the *Iowa Assessments* and its goals and purpose are significantly updated. Furthermore, despite updates and improvements, two facts remain: (a) high performance on a grade-level achievement test does not reveal when or how students learned the material (they may have started out the year already knowing the content); and (b) high performance on a grade-level achievement test doesn't tell the teacher what the advanced student is ready to learn next. Nonetheless, high performance on a grade-level test does reveal who is ready for above-level testing (Lupkowski-Shoplik,

Benbow, Assouline, & Brody, 2003; Olszewski-Kubilius, 2004; Stanley, 2005).

Above- and Off-Level Assessment

Out-of-level and *off-level* are synonymous terms that refer to going below or above the student's typical grade level. When students struggle, there is often frustration. To appropriately diagnose and/or intervene, teachers may need to go *below* grade level to find the test items that will give them useful information for placement and programming.

When students are advanced, they typically will answer correctly all, or nearly all, of the items on a grade-level test. This kind of information about a learner is helpful for determining mastery, but cannot provide sufficient information for the teacher to know what his or her students are ready to learn next. However, there is an option for teachers known as above-level testing. Since the early 1980s, several university-based gifted education centers (see Appendix C) have implemented above-level testing programs (Assouline & Lupkowski-Shoplik, 2011), which serve hundreds of thousands of students each and every year. This hugely popular out-of-school opportunity for above-level testing is largely unused in schools. Although educators distribute the talent search information about the above-level testing to their students, Olszewski-Kubilius and Lee (2005) found that less than 10% of the educators in their sample used talent search information to program for their students. This unused information could be very helpful in assisting educators in knowing who is ready for more advanced work, as well as who is ready for an accelerated approach.

21st Century Assessments

We are now in the digital age and 21st century assessments are clearly a reflection of this reality. The first computer-adaptive test to be discussed is the Measure of Academic Progress

(MAP). MAP was released in 2005, and thus is a relatively "old" test compared to the three tests scheduled for release in the 2014–2015 academic year: Smarter Balanced, PARCC, and ACT ASPIRE™. All four tests are discussed below.

Measure of Academic Progress (MAP)

The Measure of Academic Progress (MAP) test, developed by the Northwest Evaluation Association (NWEA), was one of the first computer-adaptive tests to be used on a large-scale basis. MAP assessments are similar to traditional assessments in that they correspond to state-based standards and assess in the traditional areas of reading, math, and language arts. However, the MAP assessments have at least two advantages over the more traditional paper and pencil measures of achievement. First, the tests are adaptive. In other words, they are built upon a statistical process known as Item Response Theory (IRT). The item difficulty adjusts to the student's response. Second, the tests were designed to be used up to four times during an academic year. Finally, although the MAP tests were developed relatively recently (2005), NWEA was incorporated in 1977 and has a very strong reputation among educators.

Smarter Balanced, PARCC, and ACT ASPIRE

Twenty-first century language is being replaced by references to the "next generation." Smarter Balanced Assessment Consortium and the Partnership for Assessment of Readiness for College and Careers (PARCC) are two separate multistate consortia that each received funding from the U.S. Department of Education to develop assessments that align to the Common Core State Standards, especially with respect to the universal screening of all students.

Smarter Balanced Assessment Consortium is a state-led consortium working to develop assessments that are aligned to the CCSS. The web-based resources include the alignment of the CCSS to International Baccalaureate, the Texas College Career

Readiness Standards, depth of knowledge, and breadth of coverage within a domain. To learn more about the consortium's progress on developing assessments for the standards, visit http://www.smarterbalanced.org/sample-items-and-performance-tasks.

The Partnership for Assessment of Readiness for College and Careers is a 24-state consortium that has been formed to develop a common assessment system to measure the CCSS. To learn more about its work and the progress of its assessment development, visit http://www.parcconline.org/about-parcc.

ACT ASPIRE is a longitudinal assessment program that tracks progress from elementary grades through high school with a focus on college and career readiness. ACT ASPIRE offers tests in the same areas provided by ACT's current suite of assessments in English, math, reading, and science, beginning with grade 2 and continuing through high school. ACT ASPIRE is designed for alignment with the Common Core State Standards, as well as with ACT's College Readiness Benchmarks, which have been a standard for talent search organizations in generating recommendations for participants. For more information about the ACT ASPIRE system, visit http://www.discoveractaspire.org/.

Summary

In presenting this information on assessment, we are suggesting that students and teachers are likely to benefit from a comprehensive approach to assessment. Preassessment has an important place at the table. So, too, does informal assessment of the learner's understanding of the material presented in the LE. Formal assessment procedures are catching up with the ever-changing world of computer hardware and software and now reflect the impact of technology in terms of delivery of items, as well as with regard to reporting of results.

Today's educators have a variety of options. There are many tests that have been developed by large-scale testing companies that can provide valuable insight and information into the individual learner's need as well as an understanding of that learner's needs within the context of a class of students. These assessments are valid and reliable; however, the usefulness rests with the educator who must connect the information to the learner's needs.

Chapter 4

Differentiated Learning Experiences

One of the ways of connecting to each learner's strengths and weaknesses is by differentiating learning experiences. Differentiation may occur when teachers understand standards within and across domains so they may appropriately enrich, pace, and accelerate the curriculum based on assessment data. As an example, we decided to differentiate the learning experiences within one mathematics learning progression that includes the domains of Measurement and Data (grades K–5) and Statistics and Probability (grades 6–high school). There were several reasons that we felt that this learning progression was particularly important.

First, this learning progression is frequently not addressed within elementary and secondary mathematics classrooms, even with the CCSSM, and is often isolated within a separate course. Therefore, students may not experience the important concepts within these domains until they reach high school.

Second, this learning progression can be interwoven throughout the elementary, middle, high school, and even more advanced postsecondary courses. It provides coherence and comprehensiveness to the curriculum, lending itself to broader themes, issues, and problems—a foundation for the development of curriculum for gifted and advanced learners.

Third, this learning progression provides many opportunities for differentiation. It can be integrated into other core subject areas. For example, within these sample learning experiences, data are collected to examine plant growth and the habitat of fish (science), identify preferred social activities (social studies), design map scales (social studies), and predict performance in physical fitness activities (health). Because of these opportunities for interdisciplinary study, teachers across disciplines might also be able to develop problems for students that require multiple perspectives and quantitative solutions. Moreover, using this sequence of learning experiences, the teacher can view the entire scope of content across grade levels and insert more above-level concepts into their lessons based on student readiness. As an example, students who understand fractions as numbers and are ready to apply and extend their previous understandings of operations on whole numbers (see the Number and Operations: Fractions domain) will also be ready to measure to the nearest fraction rather than whole unit or represent data using line plots as opposed to bar graphs.

Fourth, this learning progression can culminate in a discipline or career. Students who become passionate about statistics and probability can continue studying this area in their higher education courses and might even pursue a doctoral degree and ultimately work within medical, environmental, industrial, governmental, or academic fields.

Finally, the field of statistics and probability is important for being an informed citizen and interpreting data. Each individual needs to know how to examine information on a daily basis in order to determine whether the data is trustworthy, whether it has been analyzed correctly, and whether the conclusions drawn from the data are clear and sound.

Reading the Learning Experience Tables

Each of the learning experiences within this chapter includes the following components. (*Note:* The italics used on the learning experiences show how the examples differ for advanced students.)

Identified scope of the standard's expectations for each grade level. As noted by the Common Core Standards Writing Team (2011), students in grades K–5 work with data, which builds foundations for their study of statistics and probability in middle school and beyond. In these learning experiences, the focus is on measurement and data. Kindergarten students organize items into groups, count and measure objects, and label categories. In grades 1–5, students focus on representing and interpreting data by making repeated measurements and creating bar graphs, pictographs, and line-plot graphs to represent their data. Complexity is incorporated within each of the LEs through the types of mathematical problems posed, the creation of instruments, the collection of more than one set of data, the inclusion of fractions in the scale, the use of mathematical vocabulary in describing and interpreting the data, the manipulation of the data, and the implementation of interventions. At the middle school level, the students interpret their data and predictions. At grade 6, students begin to use descriptive statistics, such as mean and interquartile range. By eighth grade and beyond, students understand different types of models and functions, including linear models and relative frequency. Students make decisions and predictions based on data.

Brief description of the learning experience. Each LE is preceded by a description of how the learning experience is similar for both typical and advanced students and how it varies. Extensions are also included, which teachers may elect to use as time permits. Some of the LEs provide opportunities for interdisciplinary studies with problems involving science, health, and social studies.

Sequence of activities within each learning experience. The sequence of activities is described for typical and for advanced students. Activities that are different for advanced students are italicized for easy reference. In elementary and middle school grades, advanced and typical students have opportunities to share their data in small and whole groups. In this way, all students have opportunities for communicating and critiquing one another's work.

Implementation. The teacher is provided with specific ways to implement the learning experience in this section, which includes the use of assessments, whole-group discussions, homogeneous grouping, partner and independent work, and pacing.

Formative assessment. The final section in the learning experiences includes suggestions for preassessment and ongoing assessments. The types of assessments discussed in the LEs are informal and provide questions that might be asked during observations, in discussions, and on teacher-constructed tests or rubrics.

Throughout all of the learning experiences, the Standards of Mathematical Practice are considered. For example, students use measurement data to make sense of problems (Standard 1), reason quantitatively to answer questions regarding their data (Standard 2), meet in small and whole groups to discuss their conclusions and critique the conclusions of other students (Standard 3), and use a variety of tools to collect data and construct graphs (Standards 5, 6, and 7).

Sample Activities Aligned With the Common Core State Standards for Mathematics

Subject: Math Learning Progression
Domain: Measurement and Data (Grades K–5)

Grade K Problem **Represent and interpret data** **Standard: K.MD.2.** Directly compare two objects with a measurable attribute in common, to see which object has "more of"/"less of" the attribute and describe the difference.	**Both typical and advanced students create different groupings. Both groups may identify attributes using color, size, conceptual categories, and/or string and/or rulers for measureable attributes. Typical students group concrete items such as buttons, foods, animals, attribute blocks, 3–D objects (or objects that might be measured).** *Advanced students conceptualize groups more abstractly that may include combinations of numbers such as even, odd, prime, less than a particular number and more than a particular number, etc. (e.g., 5, 25, 55, 125, 0, 20, 50, 9, 3, 59, 44). They include groupings with more than one attribute and are able to make comparisons across groups.*
	Typical
	1. Tell the students that they will be sorting objects and pictures into different groups. Tell them that they may also use the rulers and/or strings to measure the objects. At the end of the lesson, they will create a graph together to show how many groups they created. 2. Give each student a sack with pictures and 3–D shapes to sort, rulers and/or strings for measurement, and a tally card. Use 3–D shapes and *continued*
	Advanced
	1. Tell the students that they will be sorting objects and pictures into different groups. Tell them that they will also use the rulers and/or strings to measure the objects. At the end of the lesson, they will create a graph together to show how many groups they created. 2. Give each student a sack with symbols such as *numbers* and 3–D shapes to sort, rulers and/or strings for measurement, and a tally card. Use 3–D shapes and *continued*

Grade K Problem, *continued*

pictures that can be sorted in multiple ways (e.g., foods, animals, attribute blocks, spheres of different colors).

3. Have the students place the objects or pictures in more than one pile.
4. Observe and record how the students are sorting their objects and pictures. Move around the room and ask these questions:
   a. Tell me why you placed these pictures or objects in this group.
   b. Which group has the most (or more)?
   c. Which group has the least (or less)?
   d. Which groups have the same number?
   e. Is there another way that you might group these pictures or objects?
5. While observing, encourage the students to regroup their objects or pictures and make as many groups as possible. They will keep track of the number of groups by marking their tally sheet.
6. Following the sorting of objects or pictures, in whole group, discuss the different types of groupings that were made and then create a bar graph that represents the number of groupings that the students found. Ask the students: What was the most number of groups formed? What was the least number of groups formed? Ask the students, how many groups were formed?

symbols that can be sorted in multiple ways (e.g., *attribute blocks, single-, double- and triple-digit numbers*).

3. Have the students place the objects or *symbols/numbers* in more than one pile.
4. Observe and record how the students are sorting their objects and numbers. Move around the room and ask these questions:
   a. Tell me why you placed these pictures or objects in this group.
   b. Which group has the most (or more)?
   c. Which group has the least (or less)?
   d. Which groups have the same number?
   e. Is there another way that you might group these pictures or objects?
5. While observing, encourage the students to regroup their objects or *symbols* and make as many groups as possible. They will keep track of the number of groups by marking their tally sheet.
6. Following the sorting of objects or symbols in whole group, discuss the different types of groupings that were made. Ask the students how they might share the data with other students. *Have the students create bar (or other types of) graphs that represent the number of groupings that the students found prior to the whole-group discussion.*
7. In the whole group, ask the students: how did they form their groups? What was the most number of groups formed? What was the least number of groups formed? Ask the students, how many groups were formed?

Grade K Problem, *continued*	
Implementation	
	Begin by telling the students that they will be grouping objects, pictures, and/or numbers/symbols. Show the students the contents of one of the bags and how they might use the ruler and/or the string to measure objects to identify different ways to group. Also show them how to use the tally card to keep track of how many groups they form. Based on your preassessment, pass out bags that contain the symbols to the more advanced students. You may have the students work in pairs or individually. As the students sort objects, walk around the room, asking questions, and marking your record form to identify the types and quality of the groupings (see below in the assessment section). With the advanced students, discuss ways that they might represent the data, allowing them to create their own bar (or other types of) graphs. Following the sorting activity, bring the students together in a whole group to discuss the different ways that they sorted, to create the bar graph, to answer questions regarding the bar graph, and to share other ways that the advanced students may have represented their data.

Formative Assessment	
Typical	**Advanced**
Pre- and ongoing assessment: Observe students as they measure and sort shapes and pictures. Do they use one attribute, two attributes, or more attributes to sort? In what ways do they describe how they sorted objects? Are their descriptions concrete or abstract (e.g., pumpkin vs. fruit)? How accurately do they describe "more of" or "less of" using attributes?	**Pre- and ongoing assessment:** Observe students as they measure and sort shapes, pictures, *and/or symbols*. Do the students use *more than one attribute* to sort shapes? In what ways do they describe how they sorted objects? Are their descriptions *abstract* (e.g., transportation vs. truck; odd vs. the name of the number)? *How many attributes are used in describing "more of" or "less of" a particular attribute or more than one attributes? How do they represent the data (labels on the x-axis and y-axis)? In what ways do the students compare groups? Were any particularly creative sorting methods used?*

Subject: Math Learning Progression
Domain: Measurement and Data (Grades K–5)

Grade 1 Problem	Both typical and advanced students survey their classmates. The typical students use survey information to develop a bar graph and answer questions.
Represent and interpret data. **Standard: 1.MD.4.** Organize, represent, and interpret data with up to three categories: ask and answer questions about the total number of data points, how many in each category, and how many more or less are in one category than in another.	*Advanced students pose their own questions, create a survey, gather information, develop bar graphs, and make comparisons across all graphs.*

Typical	Advanced
1. Tell the students that they are going to be learning more about their classmates and how to organize and answer questions about the information. 2. Have the students survey the students in their small group about their classmates' pets. The survey will include these questions: Do you have any pets? What kind of pets do you have? How many of each kind do you have?	1. Tell the students that they are going to have an opportunity to learn more about their classmates' interests and how to organize and answer questions about the information. 2. *Have the students create a survey to find out more about their classmates. Tell them that the survey might identify their classmates' favorite foods (e.g., pizza, hamburger, French fries), sports (e.g., soccer, baseball, tag), colors, activities at recess, subject in school (e.g., math, reading, art), or something else that the students might identify. Allow them to pose their own questions.*
	continued
continued	

Grade 1 Problem, *continued*

3. In small groups, have the students gather information about one another.
4. Following the data gathering, bring the small groups together and ask each of the group leaders to tell you the types of pets each group identified. (You could limit the number of pets to "dogs," "cats," and "others.") As the students tell you the names of the pets, write the name of the pet on the horizontal or x-axis.
5. Next have the small group leader tell you the number of each type of pet the group identified. Create a tally for each pet as the groups report.
6. Place numbers on the y-axis in equal units of one, and show the students how to create a bar graph that shows the number of each type of pet.
7. Ask the students: How many children own dogs, cats? What pet is owned by the most number of children? What pet is owned by the least?

3. In small groups, have the students gather information about one another.
4. *Following the data gathering, have each of the small groups create one or more graphs to represent the data. Have them organize the data into one or more different types of graphs: bar graph, picture graph, line graph.*
5. The advanced students join the typical students in a class discussion of the graphs that all groups have created. *Ask the students: How many children like _____? Which one is liked by the most children? Which one is liked by the least? In looking at all of the graphs, which one was liked by the most children? Which one was liked by the least? How many in our class have pets? How many like both _____ and _____ ?*

Implementation

Based on your preassessment, put the students into homogeneous groups. Those who already know how to create graphs would be in the advanced groups. Those who do not understand how to graph would be in the typical groups. Tell the entire class that they will be creating graphs to organize information about their classmates. Some of the groups will be identifying information about pets, others will be gathering information about other areas such as favorite foods, colors, or sports. Explain how to survey within the small group. For the typical learners, you might have a student who is a group leader ask the questions, while each of the students

continued

Grade 1 Problem, *continued*

writes the type and number of their pets on individual cards. For the advanced learners, you might have them identify the type of information they want to gather about their classmates, create their own surveys, and then graph the results. While the advanced learners are working independently, bring the typical learners together as a small group and graph the results of their survey. Then add the advanced learners to the group. Have the typical learners share their pet information and then have the advanced learners share their graphs with the other students. Ask questions that compare information across all of the graphs.

Formative Assessment	Typical	Advanced
	Preassessment: Design a preassessment for the whole class that presents a table of information to the students for them to interpret. For example, the table might show how the students travel to school (e.g., walking, bicycle, car, bus). Have them answer questions about the table that includes: How many children go to school by bus? By car? What way do most of the children travel to school? What way do the least number of children travel to school? **Ongoing assessment:** Did the students gather data? Did they create a bar graph to represent the data? Were they able to identify the number that is represented by each bar?	**Preassessment:** For those students who are able to interpret the graph, have them create a graph from information that you give them. For example, give them these data: After school, 5 students play video games, 3 students read, 4 students do their homework, and 7 students watch television. **Ongoing assessment:** Were they able to formulate questions to survey? Were they able to create surveys that related to their questions? Were they able to gather data? Were they able to compare results? To assess the advanced learners' graphs, observe the presence of these characteristics: bars/pictures show the correct data, labels on the x- and y-axis are labeled and correct, and intervals are equal.

Subject: Math Learning Progression
Domain: Measurement and Data (Grades K–5)

Grade 2 Problem	This is an interdisciplinary problem that involves social studies and math. Both typical and advanced students create line-plot graphs. Typical students create a line-plot graph to the nearest inch/centimeter by measuring the same map multiple times.
Represent and interpret data. **Standard: 2.MD.9.** Generate measurement data by measuring lengths of several objects to the nearest whole unit, or by making repeated measurements of the same object. Show the measurements by making a line plot, where the horizontal scale is marked off in whole-number units.	*Advanced students create line-plot graphs to the nearest half-inch by measuring two maps multiple times and making comparisons. As an extension, they may also create a scale map using the data.*

Typical	Advanced
1. Tell the students that they will be creating a line-plot to show and compare the distances on a map. 2. Give each of the students a map of the contiguous United States, a ruler, colored pencils or markers, and a blank graph with numbers on the *y*-axis and slash marks on the *x*-axis for recording.	1. Tell the students that they will be creating a line-plot to show and compare the distances on *maps*. 2. Give each of the students a map of the contiguous United States *and a map of Australia*, a ruler, colored pencils or markers, and *two blank graphs* with numbers on the *y*-axis and slash marks on the *x*-axis for recording. Both maps need to have the same scale.
continued	*continued*

Grade 2 Problem, *continued*

3. Have them draw the longest line they can draw between but within the borders of the contiguous United States. Have them measure the line segment to the nearest inch/centimeter and record it on their graph using the color name or the color itself. (The y-axis will show the numbers of inches/centimeters and the x-axis will show the color of the line drawn.) As needed, assist the students in plotting their points.

4. Have them repeat step #3 by drawing at least 7 more lines using different colors for each.

5. After they complete their measurements, they will then draw a line that connects the points on their line-plot graph.

6. Discuss the graphs with the students in whole group: How far apart is the longest line segment before hitting a border? How far apart is the shortest line segment? Which lines are about equal? What might you infer regarding distances on the map?

3. Have them draw the longest line they can draw between but within the borders of the contiguous United States (e.g., both EW and NS). Have them *measure the line segment to the nearest half inch/centimeter and record it on their graph using the color name or the color itself. (The y-axis will show the numbers of inches/centimeters and the x-axis will show the color of the line drawn.)*

4. Have them repeat step #3 by drawing at least 7 more lines using different colors for each.

5. Have them draw the longest line they can draw between but *within the borders of Australia. Have them measure the line segment to the nearest half inch/centimeter and record it on their graphs using the color name or the color itself. (The y-axis will show the numbers of inches/centimeters and the x-axis will show the color of the line drawn.)*

6. Have them repeat step #5 by drawing at least 7 more lines *using different colors for each.*

7. After they complete their measurements, they will then draw a line that connects the points on their line-plot graphs for the United States and for Australia.

8. Encourage the students to pose other questions they might *want to answer about differences between the United States and Australia maps (e.g., what is the shortest and longest distances along the Eastern and Western coasts?).*

continued

Grade 2 Problem, *continued*

	9. Discuss the graphs with the students in the whole group: How far apart is the longest line segment before hitting a border? How far apart is the shortest line segment? *How do the line segments on the United States and the Australia maps compare? Which one has the longest line segments? What might you infer regarding distances on the map? Address any questions that they may have posed.* 10. **Extension:** *Have the students create a scale map using the data from their plots and comparing it to actual miles or kilometers.*
Implementation	Using preassessments, determine which students will be drawing a line–plot of one country vs. two countries and will be measuring to the nearest half inch/centimeter vs. inch/centimeter. Tell the students that they will be learning about representing data using a line–plot graph. Next describe the task and then distribute the materials to each student. Have the students work independently. Variation in rate differences among students might be accommodated by having students draw more or fewer lines on the map. More copies of maps that have the same scale might be available for additional lines. After the students have completed their graphs, discuss the results with all of the students.

Formative Assessment

Typical	Advanced
Preassessment: To preassess both typical and advanced learners, design an assessment that includes measuring objects to the nearest inch/centimeter and to the nearest half inch/centimeter. Other items might compare line *continued*	**Ongoing assessment:** Did the students pose questions that related to the lines they drew on the maps? Were they able to compare line segments within the same map and across maps? *continued*

Grade 2 Problem, *continued*

segments (e.g., what is the longest or shortest line segment?) and place points on a graph that represent data that they collected by measuring objects. **Ongoing assessment:** To assess the typical and advanced learners, keep a record of their responses to the questions in small and large group: Did they represent the numerical data correctly? Were they able to measure the line segments accurately? Were they able to compare line segments?	Extensions: To assess the advanced learners' scale, observe the presence of these characteristics: key contains a symbol, includes a compass rose, represents the measurements and the miles/kilometers, and is labeled and can be read easily.

Adapted from Illustrative Mathematics. (n.d.). *2.MD. The longest walk.* Retrieved from http://www.illustrativemathematics.org/illustrations/486

Subject: Math Learning Progression
Domain: Measurement and Data (Grades K–5)

Grade 3 Problem	This interdisciplinary problem addresses both mathematics and science. Both typical and advanced students conduct research, keep science journals, measure plant growth, and create line-plot graphs.
Represent and interpret data. Standard: 3.MD.4.	*Advanced students design and conduct experiments that consider other factors that might influence plant growth.*
Generate measurement data by measuring lengths using rulers marked with halves and fourths of an inch. Show the data by making a line plot, where the horizontal scale is marked off in appropriate units—whole numbers, halves, or quarters.	

	Typical	Advanced
	1. Have each student plant a "Paperwhite Narcissus" or "Amaryllis" bulb. If space does not permit for each student to have his or her own plant, you might have several of each for the entire class. Helpful hint: You might want to plant a few extras in case a plant doesn't grow or a student is absent. *continued*	1. Have each student plant a "Paperwhite Narcissus" or "Amaryllis" bulb. If space does not permit for each student to have his or her own plant, you might have several of each for the entire class. 2. Have the students research each of the plants, their parts, and the type of environment needed for these *continued*

Grade 3 Problem, continued

2. Have the students research each of the plants, their parts, and the type of environment needed for these bulbs to bloom (see http://www.kidsgardening.org). Have the students pose questions that they would like to study.
3. Have the students prepare containers for the bulbs.
4. As the bulbs grow, students measure the height of each plant and record the measurement to the nearest quarter inch/centimeter in their scientific journal.
5. Have the students create a line plot to record the plants' growth. On the y-axis, have them list the inches/centimeters to the nearest quarter unit. On the x-axis, have them list the days of the week/month.
6. Have them create hypotheses about the plant's growth: What height will the plant be tomorrow? Next week? Next month?
7. Following the maturation of the plant, meet with the students in whole group and discuss the results from their scientific journals, their graphs, and any experiments that might have been implemented. Were their hypotheses accurate? What might have influenced the results? What did you learn about growing flowering plants inside?

bulbs to bloom (see http://www.kidsgardening. org). Have the students pose questions that they would like to study.
3. Have the students prepare containers for the bulbs. *Have students record the exact measurements of the amount of pebbles, size of drainage holes, and soil. Students will pose questions and vary these factors as needed to address their questions. For example: Plants with ___ amount of pebbles grow taller than plants without ___ amount of pebbles. Plants with ___ type of soil grow better than plants with ___ type of soil. Ask students, what if you don't have an opportunity to collect data every day? What might you do?*
4. *As the bulbs grow, have the students record the water they used and any other contributing factors such as sunlight, temperature in the room. Have the students pose hypotheses using the contributing factors: Plants with ___ amount of water grow taller than plants with ___ amount of water; Plants that are placed in the sunlight grow taller than plants that are away from the sunlight. Students measure the height of each plant and record the measurement to the nearest quarter inch/ centimeter in their scientific journal.*
5. Have the students create a line plot to record the plants' growth. On the y-axis, have them list the
continued

Grade 3 Problem, *continued*

inches/centimeters to the nearest quarter unit. On the x-axis, have them list the days of the week/month.

6. Have them create hypotheses about the plant's growth: What height will the plant be tomorrow? Next week? Next month? *What conditions appear to influence the plant's growth such as water, light, soil, pebbles, or drainage? Students may also want to discuss linear growth relative to variability in growth.*

7. Following the maturation of the plant, meet with the students in whole group and discuss the results from their scientific journals, their graphs, and any experiments that might have been implemented. Were their hypotheses accurate? *What factors contributed to the growth of the plants? If you were growing more plants, what would you do based on your results?*

Implementation

Each of the students will conduct research and prepare containers for the bulbs. Following this initial preparation, the teacher will describe how to measure the plant, keep their scientific journals, and maintain their graphs. Students pose questions that they would like to study. The advanced students will pose questions about other factors that might influence the growth of their plant. These students might create hypotheses for more controlled experiments. Given the number of possible variables that might affect the growing plant (e.g., pebble to soil ratio, amount of sunlight, amount of water), the teacher might want to pair or group the advanced students and have them select one of the variables to study. Following their studies, they might put their data together to describe "optimal" growing conditions for the plant. Throughout the period that this project continues, set aside time to explore questions about the plants, allowing the students to make inferences and draw conclusions. At the end of the project, discuss the students' graphs with the whole group.

Grade 3 Problem, *continued*		
Formative Assessment	Typical	Advanced
	Preassessment: Using observations and questioning, determine which students are ready to consider multiple variables that might influence the growth of a plant. This assessment might be through observations of classroom behavior during the early stages of this experiment (e.g., To what degree did the students research the plants? What questions did the students pose following their research?). **Ongoing assessment:** To assess the students' graphs, ask these questions: Did they measure the plant accurately? Did they represent the numerical data on the graph correctly? Were they able to compare plant growth across different types of bulbs, from day to day, and from week to week? Were they able to predict plant growth? To assess the students' journals, ask these questions: Did they make an entry on a daily basis? Did the entry include a measurement of the plant growth? Did they record other variables that might have affected the plants' growth such as sunlight and water?	**Ongoing assessment:** To assess the advanced learners' experiments, observe the presence of these characteristics in their scientific journals: Did the question include two variables (e.g., growth and sunlight or growth and amount of pebbles or growth and amount of water)? Did they record and measure the second variable (e.g., sunlight, water) along with the plant's growth? Did they make accurate predictions based on their observations? Were their conclusions based on the data they collected?

Subject: Math Learning Progression
Domain: Measurement and Data (Grades K–5)

Grade 4 Problem	This interdisciplinary problem addresses both mathematics and health. Both typical and advanced students predict results, collect data on physical activities that are performed in 10-second and 30-second intervals, make a line plot to display the data (using fractions), and interpret the results.
Represent and interpret data. **Standard: 4.MD.4.** Make a line plot to display a data set of measurements in fractions of a unit (e.g., 1/2, 1/4, 1/8). Solve problems involving addition and subtraction of fractions by using information presented in line plots.	*Advanced students demonstrate a variety of ways to represent the data (using fractions and/or decimals), interpret results, and consider the effects of extreme values. Extensions include extending the physical competition to other classes and recording the results.*

Typical	Advanced
1. Tell the students that they will be participating in a fourth-grade physical fitness contest. Each student will collect data on (a) number of sit-ups in 10 seconds and in 30 seconds, (b) number of jumping jacks in 10 seconds and in 30 seconds and (c) the length of a sprint in 10 seconds and in 30 seconds. Demonstrate each of the activities. Hint: Collect the data but use numbers to represent students rather than student names to ensure anonymity. *continued*	1. Tell the students that they will be participating in a fourth-grade physical fitness contest. Each student will collect data on (a) number of sit-ups in 10 seconds and in 30 seconds, (b) number of jumping jacks in 10 seconds and in 30 seconds, and (c) the length of a sprint in 10 seconds and in 30 seconds. Demonstrate each of the activities. 2. Ask the students to predict how many and how many times they might be able to do the activity in 10 seconds and 30 seconds and how far they might *continued*

Grade 4 Problem, *continued*	
2. Ask the students to predict how many and how many times they might be able to do the activity in 10 seconds and 30 seconds and how far they might be able to sprint in 10 seconds and 30 seconds. 3. Show the students the timers and the data recording sheets that they will be using that includes a place to record the student's number, the number of completed jumping jacks/sit-ups or length of the jump, and the time unit (10 seconds and 30 seconds). Model the data collection procedures. 4. Divide the students into pairs and have the students collect the data on their partner in the classroom (for the jumping jacks and sit ups) and then go outside on the school track (for the sprints). If you do not have enough stopwatches, you could act as a stopwatch by verbally telling the students when to start and when to stop. 5. Have the students meet in small groups of four to six and organize their data for each activity from least to most for the jumping jacks/sit-ups and the longest to the shortest. (Fractions up to 1/8 should be included for the sprint.) Have them order the data individually and then in small groups for assessment purposes. Give each of the groups additional data sheets to help them organize their data. The data sheet will have a column to put all of *continued*	be able to sprint in 10 seconds and 30 seconds. *Ask them to predict the range for their class and the range for all of the fourth-grade classes.* 3. Show the students the timers and the data recording sheets that they will be using that includes a place to record the student's number, the number of completed jumping jacks/sit-ups or length of the jump, and the time unit (10 seconds and 30 seconds). Model the data collection procedures. 4. Divide the students into pairs and have the students collect the data on their partner in the classroom (for the jumping jacks and sit ups) and then go outside on the school track (for the sprints). If you do not have enough stopwatches, you could act as a stopwatch by verbally telling the students when to start and when to stop. 5. Have the students meet in small groups of four to six and organize their data for each activity from least to most for the jumping jacks/sit-ups and the longest to the shortest. *(Decimals and/or fractions up to 1/8 should be included for the sprint.)* Have them order the data individually and then in a group for assessment purposes. Give each of the groups additional data sheets to help them organize their data. The data sheet will have a column to put all of the students' numbers and columns for 10 seconds *continued*

Grade 4 Problem, *continued*

the students' numbers and columns for 10 seconds and for 30 seconds for each of the activities (e.g., jumping jacks, sit-ups, and sprints).

6. Next bring the students together in a whole group to organize all of their data from the least to most and the shortest to longest. Record the data on a combined class record form with all of the students' numbers in one column, a column for the jumping jacks, a column for the sit-ups, and a column for the sprints. Each of the activity columns will be subdivided into 10-second and 30-second columns. Ask these questions as the data are being organized: What was the farthest distance sprinted in 10 seconds and in 30 seconds? What was the greatest number of jumping jacks/sit-ups completed in 10 seconds and in 30 seconds? What is the range (e.g., the greatest and the least values) in your group? In the class? What was the most frequent number of jumping jacks? How accurate was your prediction about your performance?

7. Create a line plot graph (with number or length on the y-axis and numbers of students on the x-axis). Create a line plot for each of the activities. Discuss further by making comparisons across graphs. What would be your prediction of how far each

continued

---

and for 30 seconds for each of the activities (e.g., jumping jacks, sit-ups, and sprints).

6. *Have the students identify possible ways that they might represent the data. In examining their data, they might elect to use bar graphs, pictographs, or line graphs.*

7. Next bring the students together in a whole group to organize all of their data from the least to most and the shortest to the longest. Record the data on a combined class record form with all of the students' numbers in one column, a column for the jumping jacks, a column for the sit-ups, and a column for the sprints. Each of the activity columns will be subdivided into 10-second and 30-second columns. Ask these questions as the data are being organized: What was the farthest distance sprinted in 10 seconds and in 30 seconds? What was the greatest number of jumping jacks/sit-ups completed in 10 seconds and in 30 seconds? What is the range (e.g., the greatest and the least values) in your group? *Why do you think there is a difference? Were there any extreme values? Which distance was run the most? What was the most frequent number of jumping jacks? How accurate was your prediction about your performance? About your class's performance? If students have knowledge of central tendency, a sixth-grade standard, you might*

continued

Grade 4 Problem, *continued*

could do the activity in 5 minutes and in one hour? Compare sit-ups with jumping jacks. Which one was easier for the students? Which activity appeared to have the greatest range? Explain your answer.

ask: *What are the mean, median, and mode for students in your group vs. students in our class for each activity? Which measure most accurately describes the data? What would happen to the mean, median, and mode if you excluded those?*

8. *Have the students share the ways that they could represent the data.*

9. Create a line plot graph (with number or length on the y-axis and numbers of students on the x-axis). Create a line plot for each of the activities. Discuss further by making comparisons across graphs. What would be your prediction of how far each could do the activity in 5 minutes and in one hour? Compare sit-ups with jumping jacks. Which one was easier for the students? Which activity appeared to have the greatest range? Explain your answer.

10. ***Extension:*** *Have the students create posters so that other classes might participate in the fitness competition. Invite other students to submit their data to the class for further analysis by comparing the new data to the already collected data. Have the class analyze these data using measures of central tendency and report the results to the class. The students might also use the President's Physical Fitness test for students K–12, which is frequently administered during physical education classes. Students might use the collected data to examine the number or percentage of students who might earn a certificate on the test.*

Grade 4 Problem, *continued*

Implementation

The teacher will announce to the students that they will have an opportunity to participate in a fourth-grade physical fitness contest. This announcement might be in the form of a letter from a coach, a school administrator, or even a state/government agency. The teacher will demonstrate each of the activities and model how the students are to collect data. The teacher will encourage the students to make predictions about their performance and/or the class performance. After the students collect data, they will meet in small groups to organize the data from most to least or farthest to shortest. The advanced group of students will identify ways that the data might be represented. They might use fractions or decimals to represent the length of the sprint. In the whole group, the data will be reorganized using the entire class. The advanced students will share their ideas for representing the data. A line plot graph will be developed using the data. For the advanced students, discussion questions will address predictions, the effects of extreme scores, and (for those students who are ready for sixth-grade standards) mean, median, and range.

Formative Assessment

Typical	Advanced
Preassessment: Determine which students are able to order fractions and/or convert fractions to decimals. Using observations and questioning, determine which students are able to make realistic predictions and are ready to represent data in multiple ways (e.g., bar graphs, pictographs, line graphs). Identify which students know measures of central tendency. **Ongoing assessment:** To assess the students' organization of data, examine each of the student's data sheets to determine if they *continued*	**Ongoing assessment:** To assess the line-plot graphs and the extension activity, observe the presence of these characteristics: Did they measure the length accurately? Did they measure the frequency correctly? Were they able to order the fractions/decimals? Were they able to identify several ways of representing the data? Did they represent the numerical data correctly? Where they able to compare across physical activities? Were they able to use mathematical vocabulary in making comparisons (e.g., mean, median, mode, range)? Did they describe the effects of extreme values?

Grade 4 Problem, *continued*

are able to order data from least to most and from longest to shortest.

To assess the line-plot graphs, observe the presence of these characteristics: Did they measure the length accurately? Did they measure the frequency correctly? Were they able to order the fractions? Did they represent the numerical data on the graph correctly? Where they able to compare across physical activities?

Subject: Math Learning Progression
Domain: Measurement and Data (Grades K–5)

Grade 5 Problem	Both typical and advanced students predict results, collect data on fluency in basic facts, create a line plot to display the data (using fractions), and interpret the results.
Represent and interpret data. **Standard: 5.MD.2.** Make a line plot to display a data set of measurements in fractions of a unit (e.g., 1/2, 1/4, 1/8). Use operations on fractions for this grade to solve problems involving information presented in line plots.	*Advanced students create a double/triple line-plot graph and make comparisons, discussing trends. They also plan and implement possible interventions to improve student performance in mathematical fluency in their classroom with one or more students.*

Typical	Advanced
1. Explain that the students in Granbury School are preparing for a math state assessment and want to improve their overall performance on basic facts. They have been practicing their facts for one week. Provide the students with student data that represent the number of correct solutions of one-digit multiplication problems that one student from the class solved. If the student were to get all of the answers correct, he or she would have solved 100 problems in one minute. *continued*	1. Explain that the students in Granbury School are preparing for a math state assessment and want to improve their overall performance on basic facts. They have been practicing their facts for one week. Provide the students with student data that represent the number of correct solutions of one-digit multiplication problems that one student from the class solved. If the student were to get all of the answers correct, he or she would have solved 100 problems in one minute. *continued*

Grade 5 Problem, *continued*

2. From the graphs that they know how to create, ask the students to develop several ways of graphing the data. Tell them they want to make sure that they represent the data accurately.

3. Have the students share the ways that they graphed their data.

4. Have them answer these questions: Describe what happened to the student's performance from Monday through Friday. Did it increase, decrease, or stay the same? What was the range of the student's performance? Predict how the student might perform next week.

5. Divide the students into homogenous groups based on their understandings and misunderstandings of ways of representing data. For students who were unable to create a line plot graph, you will want to help them understand how to convert the data into fractions, create a scale, and plot the data.

6. Give this group another set of data to plot for one student from Granbury School.

7. Have all of the students share their graphs as a whole group. Describe what happened to the student's performance from Monday through Friday. Did it increase, decrease, or stay the same? What was the range of the student's performance?

continued

2. From the graphs that they know how to create, ask the students to develop several ways of graphing the data. Tell them they want to make sure that they represent the data accurately.

3. Have the students share the ways that they graphed their data. *The students may share many ways of graphing but you will be looking for those students who created a graph that includes a title and displays fractional/decimal data on the y-axis and the days of the week on the x-axis.*

4. Have them answer these questions: Describe what happened to the student's performance from Monday through Friday. Did it increase, decrease, or stay the same? What was the range of the student's performance? *What were the student's mean, median, mode, and range of performance?* Predict how the student might perform next week. *Describe the trend.*

5. Since these students will have been able to create graphs, they will be able to plot and compare data from other students using the same graph. *Give them additional sets of data to plot for two or more fictitious students from Granbury School. You might also have them convert their fractions to decimals if they have that knowledge.*

continued

Grade 5 Problem, *continued*

What were the student's mean, median, mode, and range of performance? Predict how the student might perform next week.

8. Have the advanced students share some of the possible interventions with the whole class for these students and for their classmates if they are working on improving their basic fact fluency. If one or more students would like to improve their fluency, have them try one of these interventions and plot their data to share.

6. Now have them compare performance across students. What was the range of the students' performance? What was the students' mean, median, mode, and range of performance? Predict how each of the students might perform next week. Describe the trend for each student.

7. Now share student performance data for the next week. Have them graph these data. Were the predictions correct for each student? What was the range of the students' performance? What was the students' mean, median, mode, and range of performance? How did the students' performance compare to the previous week? Draw conclusions regarding their performance. Describe the trend for each student. Have them discuss possible interventions to improve the students' performance (e.g., practice at home, flash cards, partner practice).

8. Have them share this information with the rest of the class in a group discussion.

9. *Extension:* If the class is also trying to improve its fluency with basic facts, the advanced students might test one or more of the suggested interventions. The advanced students would then share the results with the rest of the class.

Implementation

Begin the lesson by providing data to all of the students for them to graph. Move around the room looking at how each of the students is creating graphs to represent the data. After a brief discussion, use the data to

continued

Grade 5 Problem, *continued*		

homogeneously group students around their instructional needs. Work with those students who are unable to create a scale using fractions or who may not understand how to create two variables with the data. Following this small-group instruction, have these students create another graph using these data. With those students who are able to create a graph, give them additional student data to plot using the same graph. After the new data has been plotted, lead them in a small-group discussion, explaining trends. Next have them brainstorm possible interventions. Return to the instructional groups to make sure that they understand how to create graphs. Bring all of the students together for a final discussion of all of the graphs. Have students think of possible interventions and allow the advanced students to test their interventions in the classroom.

Assessment	Typical	Advanced
	Preassessment: Use observations to determine which students are able to create a line plot graph with the data that you provide. Did they label their graph correctly? Did the x-axis include the days of the week? Did the y-axis include a fractional scale? Did they plot the data correctly? **Ongoing assessment:** To assess the line-plot graphs, assess student ability in the following areas: Were they able to order the fractions/decimals to make a scale? Did they represent the numerical data on the graph correctly? Where they able to compare across students? Were they able to use mathematical vocabulary in making comparisons (e.g., mean, median, mode, range)?	**Ongoing assessment:** To assess the line-plot graphs, assess the presence of these characteristics: Were they able to order the fractions/decimals to make a scale? Did they represent the numerical data on the graph correctly? Where they able to compare across students? Were they able to use mathematical vocabulary in making comparisons (e.g., mean, median, mode, range)? Were they able to make accurate predictions and describe trends? For the advanced students' interventions, assess the presence of these characteristics: Were they able to describe performance trends? Did they plan an intervention that related to increasing mathematical fluency? Did they match the measurement to the type of data collected? Did they organize the data accurately? Did they represent the data on the graph correctly? Did they interpret the effects of the intervention correctly?

Subject: Math Learning Progression
Domain: Statistics and Probability (Grades K–12)

Grade 6 Problem	Both typical and advanced learners determine how the shape of a distribution influences measures of center and variability. Both groups calculate the mean, median, interquartile range, and mean absolute deviation of a data set and explore how changing one or more data points affects the distribution and the measures of the center. Typical students create one histogram using the original data generated by throwing the paper airplane.
Represent and interpret data. **Standard: 6.SP.5d** Summarize numerical data sets in relation to their context, such as by: relating the choices of measures of center and variability to the shape of the data distribution and the context in which the data were collected.	*Advanced students create several histograms based on the original and simulated data and compare their distributions to make generalizations about how the shape of a distribution affects measures of center.*

Typical	Advanced
1. Tell the students that they will calculate the mean, median, interquartile range, and mean absolute deviation for a data set consisting of distances that a paper airplane traveled after it was thrown. 2. Break students into groups of five or six and give each group a paper airplane. Ask each student in the group to throw the paper airplane twice and then measure the distance in units (inches or centimeters). *continued*	1. Tell the students that they will calculate the mean, median, interquartile range, and mean absolute deviation for a data set consisting of distances that a paper airplane traveled after it was thrown. 2. Break students into groups of five or six and give each group a paper airplane. Ask each student in the group to throw the paper airplane twice and then measure the distance in units (inches or centimeters). *continued*

Grade 6 Problem, *continued*

3. Have the students calculate the measures of the center and variability, record it on their data sheets, and draw a histogram of their data.
4. Ask the students the following:
   a. Can you change two distances that will keep the mean the same but change the median?
   b. What happens to the mean and mean absolute deviation when you take the shortest or longest distances out of the data set?
   c. What happens to the measures of the center and variability if you multiply the longest distance by 2?
5. Tell the students to change other data points and recalculate the mean, median, interquartile range, and mean absolute deviation, making notes about how the distributions were changed and how these changes affected these measures.

3. Have the students calculate the measures of the center and variability, record it on their data sheets, and draw a histogram of their data.
4. Ask the students the following:
   a. *Can you change two distances that will keep the mean the same but change the median?*
   b. *What happens to the mean and mean absolute deviation when you take the shortest or longest distances out of the data set? (Ask the students to draw two histograms—one with the shortest distance removed from the data set and a second with the longest distance taken out of the data.)*
   c. *What happens to the measures of the center and variability if you multiply the longest distance by 2? (Ask the students to draw a histogram with the longest distance multiplied by 2.)*
5. *Have the students compare the four histograms and answer the following questions:*
   a. *In which of the distributions is the mean a better representation of the center than the median? Why?*
   b. *When would the median be a better distribution than the mean (The mean depends on the actual values in a data set, but the median is dependent only on the relative position of the values.)?*
   c. *Which measure of variability would you use with the mean? Why?*

Grade 6 Problem, *continued*

Implementation

Based on your preassessment, put the students into homogeneous groups. Those who already know how to compare distributions and describe the measures of center in terms of the variability will be in the advanced group. Those who do not know how to do this will be in the typical learners group. Begin by telling the students that they will be recording distances that a paper airplane travels after it was thrown (decide on the units of measurement before beginning the activity). Also provide each student with a data sheet that has two columns. Tell students to record their distances in Column 1. In Column 2, write mean, median, interquartile range, and mean absolute deviation. Tell students that each group member will do the calculations independently and then come back to the small group to compare their answers. They will record their final decision in Column 2. The typical students will create one histogram and the advanced students will create multiple histograms. Divide students into groups of five or six, placing the advanced students in the same group. As the students record their data and draw their histograms, walk around the room, ask questions, and make notes about how the students are making generalizations about distributions and measures of center and variability.

Formative Assessment	Typical	Advanced
	Preassessment: Design a preassessment for the whole class that requires them to construct several histograms from data and has them make comparisons about the distributions. Have them answer questions about the distribution that include: Which distribution would have the highest mean? How do the distributions with the highest and lowest mean differ as a multiple of the *continued*	**Preassessment:** Students who are able to make comparisons about the distributions and describe measures of center and variability will create multiple histograms based on the changes they make to the original data. **Ongoing assessment:** Observe students as they create multiple histograms. *continued*

Grade 6 Problem, *continued*

mean absolute deviation? What do measures of center and variability express about distributions?

Ongoing assessment:
Observe students as they collect their data, calculate measures of center and variability, and discuss how changing the data affects these measures. Are they able to make generalizations about how the data must change to change the mean or the median? Can they extend this understanding to begin making statements about how outliers will affect measures of center and variability?

Are they able to compare them in terms of both measures of center and variability? Can they describe differences in means as a multiple of the mean absolute deviation?

Subject: Math Learning Progression
Domain: Statistics and Probability (Grades 6–12)

Grade 7 Problem	Both typical and advanced students simulate a mark-recapture experiment to determine the number of trout living in a stream. Both groups compare their sample results and use proportions to make inferences about the population. Typical students produce a reasonable estimate of the population based on their samples.
Use random sampling to draw inferences about a population. Standard: 7.SP.1	*Advanced students do the same but also create a scatterplot using their simulated data, describe how the data are clustered, and use this information to produce a more accurate estimate of the population.*
Understand that statistics can be used to gain information about a population by examining a sample of the population; generalizations about a population from a sample are valid only if the sample is representative of that population. Understand that random sampling tends to produce representative samples and support valid inferences.	
	Typical	**Advanced**
	1. Tell the students that they are going to simulate an experiment about how to use random sampling to make inferences about a population. Explain to *continued*	1. Tell the students that they are going to simulate an experiment about how to use random sampling to make inferences about a population. Explain to *continued*

Grade 7 Problem, *continued*

the students that a group of scientists captured and tagged some trout in a stream, freeing them once they were tagged. The scientists later recapture the trout in the same stream and count the number tagged. They will use the proportion of tagged to total trout to estimate the total population of trout in the stream.

2. Place the students in groups of five or six and give each group a container filled with both marked (previously tagged trout) and unmarked tokens and a data sheet. Tell the students how many total number of tokens are marked, which corresponds to the number of trout tagged.

3. Remind students of the importance of random sampling. For example, ask the following:

   a. How would you get a representative sample from a lake? (Do they consider sampling fish from different parts/depths, feeding habitats of the lake?)

   b. Describe a poor method of collecting the sample.

4. Tell them that each student in the group will grab a handful of tokens, record the total and marked number of tokens, and create the proportion of marked to total tokens. When the first student finishes, she replaces the tokens, shakes the container, and hands it to the next student who

   continued

the students that a group of scientists captured and tagged some trout in a stream, freeing them once they were tagged. The scientists later recapture the trout in the same stream and count the number tagged. They will use the proportion of tagged to total trout to estimate the total population of trout in the stream.

2. Place the students in groups of five or six and give each group a container filled with both marked (previously tagged trout) and unmarked tokens and a data sheet. Tell the students how many total number of tokens are marked, which corresponds to the number of trout tagged.

3. Remind students of the importance of random sampling. For example, ask the following:

   a. How would you get a representative sample from a lake? (Do they consider sampling fish from different parts/depths, feeding habitats of the lake?)

   b. Describe a poor method of collecting the sample.

4. Tell them that each student in the group will grab a handful of tokens, record the total and marked number of tokens, and create the proportion of marked to total tokens. When the first student finishes, she replaces the tokens, shakes the container, and hands it to the next student who

   continued

Grade 7 Problem, *continued*

repeats the process. Continue this process until the group has 20 trials.

5. Following the data gathering, provide each group with the total number of tokens in the container, then ask the groups to do the following:
   a. Solve each proportion and estimate the population for each proportion.
   b. Provide a single reasonable estimate for the population.
6. In a whole group, share each group's single estimate of the population. Ask them the following:
   a. How did you create your estimate (e.g., the students might calculate the mean and mean absolute deviation and use these to determine a reasonable estimate)?
   b. Did any of the random samples not produce good estimates?
   c. If so, why do you think the samples were not good?
   d. How does random sampling allow you to make inferences about a population?

repeats the process. Continue this process until the group has 20 trials.

5. Following the data gathering, provide each group with the total number of tokens in the container, then ask the groups to do the following:
   a. Solve each proportion and estimate the population for each proportion *(This task also addresses 7.RP.2c).*
   b. Provide a single reasonable estimate for the population.
6. *Have the students create a scatterplot of their random samples placing the number of marked tokens on the x-axis and the total number of tokens captured on the y-axis. Ask them the following about the complexion of the data:*
   a. *Does the relationship between the marked tokens and the total number of tokens appear to be positive or negative or neither?*
   b. *How much cluster is there in the data?*
   c. *Can you identify any outliers?*

continued

Grade 7 Problem, *continued*

7. In a whole group, share each group's single estimate of the population. Ask them the following:

a. How did you create your estimate (e.g., the students might calculate the mean and mean absolute deviation and use these to determine a reasonable estimate)?

b. Did any of the random samples not produce good estimates?

c. If so, why do you think the samples were not good?

d. How does random sampling allow you to make inferences about a population?

Implementation

Based on your preassessment, put the students into homogeneous groups. Those who already know how to create scatterplots would be in the advanced group. Those who do not understand how to create scatterplots would be in the typical groups. Gather–light colored tokens (e.g., chips, buttons, beans) and place a mark on about 30% of them, keeping track of the number of marked versus unmarked. Prepare several containers with approximately 100–200 tokens (don't place exactly 100 or 200 tokens in the container; rather place a total such as 168). In addition, create a Data Summary sheet that contains four columns. Column 1 should be called Total Number of Trout Captured and Marked (M). Fill in column one with the total number of tokens marked in each container. Column 2 should be called Total Count of Trout in Second Capture (C), Column 3 should be called Total Count of Marked Trout in Second Capture (R), and Column 4 should be called Estimated Trout Population (P). Tell the entire class that they will be conducting a mark–recapture experiment about how to use random sampling to make inferences about a population. Explain to the class that in this method, scientists capture members of a target species; in this case, trout. They then mark this capture and release them. After a period of time passes, a second capture is conducted and the count of marked and unmarked members is

continued

Grade 7 Problem, *continued*

recorded. The total population of the species can be estimated using the following proportion: $P/M=C/R$, where P=total population, M=total marked on the first capture, C=total number captured during the second capture, and R=number of marked on the second capture. Further explain to the class that students in the groups will take turns reaching into the container and pulling out a handful of tokens. Discuss the importance of shaking the container before each trial to ensure that they are using random sampling. As each student takes a turn, ask the student who is next to record the number of marked tokens (R) and the sample size (C). While the advanced learners are working on their scatterplot, check that the typical learners are using a good method to create their estimate of the total number of marked tokens. When the advanced learners have finished creating their scatterplot, bring all learners together in a large group. Ask questions about their graphs.

For more information about mark-recapture methods, see http://www.sitesalive.com/tg/ml/private/mltgmark.htm.

Formative Assessment	Typical	Advanced
	Preassessment: Design a preassessment for the whole class that requires them to construct a scatterplot using two continuous variables. Ask them questions about the scatterplot such as: How are the two variables related? As variable one increases, what happens to variable two? **Ongoing assessment:** Observe students as they collect their data, set up their proportions, and calculate their estimates. Did they set up the proportions correctly? Was their single estimated population reasonable? Did they identify any samples that did not provide good estimates?	**Preassessment:** Students who are able to make a scatterplot will create a scatterplot of the data from the simulated experiment. **Ongoing assessment:** Observe students as they collect their data, set up their proportions, calculate their estimates, and create their scatterplot. Did they set up the proportions correctly? Was their single estimated population reasonable? Were they able to create an accurate scatterplot of their data? Could they discuss how and why the data were clustered?

*This example has been modified from *Random Drawing Tool—Sampling Distribution*, 2008, National Council of Teachers of Mathematics, http://Illuminations.nctm.org/ActivityDetail.aspx?ID=159.

Subject: Math Learning Progression
Domain: Statistics and Probability (Grades 6–12)

Grade 8 Problem	Both typical and advanced learners create a scatterplot, describe how the pattern of dots shows the relationship between two variables, and discuss how outliers affect fit of a straight line. Typical students create a scatterplot using graph paper and fit a straight line to the data. They discuss how outliers would change how they would fit a straight line to the data.
Investigate Patterns of Association in Bivariate Data. **Standard: 8.SP.2** Know that straight lines are widely used to model relationships between two quantitative variables. For scatter plots that suggest a linear association, informally fit a straight line, and informally assess the model fit by judging the closeness of the data points to the line.	*Advanced students use Excel (or an alternate software such as Fathom® or a TI calculator) to create their scatterplot and fit a straight line to the data (create a linear model of the data) and then make changes to their data to see how these changes affect the linear model.*

Typical	Advanced
1. Tell the students that they will be creating a scatterplot using arm span as the independent or x variable and height as the dependent or y variable. 2. Students work in pairs to measure their arm span and height to the nearest centimeter. *continued*	1. Tell the students that they will be creating a scatterplot using arm span as the independent or x variable and height as the dependent or y variable. 2. Students work in pairs to measure their arm span and height to the nearest centimeter. *continued*

Grade 8 Problem, *continued*

3. Learners break into groups of six to eight and each learner creates a scatterplot using his or her group's data.	3. *Learners break into a small group and follow the instructions found on the website cited in Implementation to create a scatterplot and fit a straight line to the data (linear model). If the group of advanced learners is less than six, provide the group with additional data.*
4. Learners informally fit a straight line to their data. And answer this question: How did you decide where to place your line? Next draw an outlier on each group's graph and ask: How would this outlier change where you drew your straight line?	4. *Have the students change one pair in their data set to create an outlier. Have them use a formal definition such as an outlier exists when a data point is at least 1.5 interquartile deviations from the mean. Have them recreate their scatterplot and linear model and answer this question: How did your outlier change your linear model?*
5. In a whole group ask these questions: How are these two variables related? How do you know? How closely are the two variables related? How would your line look if the two variables were negatively related? How would your line look if the two variables had none or very little relationship?	5. *In a whole group ask these questions: How are these two variables related? How do you know? How closely are they related How would your line look if the two variables were negatively related? How would your line look if the two variables had none or very little relationship?*

Implementation

Based on your preassessment, put the students into homogeneous groups. Those who already know how to create scatterplots, fit a straight line to the data, and have a working knowledge of Excel would be in the advanced group. The rest of the students would be in the typical learners group. Create a Data Record sheet that contains two columns. Students will record their arm–span measurement in Column 1 and their height in Column 2. Explain to the students that first each student's arm–span and height will be measured to the nearest centimeter and recorded on the Data Record sheet. Next they will create a scatterplot of the two measurements, arm–span and height. After they create their scatterplot, they will fit a straight line to the data

continued

Grade 8 Problem, *continued*

and assess the model fit. Place the students in their groups. As each student is being measured, ask the student who is next to record the measurements in the proper columns. While the advanced learners are using Excel to create their scatterplot and fit their line, check that the typical learners are informally fitting a reasonably straight line to their data. When the advanced learners have finished creating their scatterplot and linear model, bring all learners together in a large group. Ask questions about their plots and lines.

Download instructions for creating a scatterplot and linear model using Excel from this website: http://www.ncsu.edu/chemistry/resource/excel/excel.html#cal. Make copies of the relevant pages (through Figure 7) for the advanced learners.

Formative Assessment	Typical	Advanced
	Preassessment: Design a preassessment that includes creating a scatterplot, fitting a straight line to the data, and using Excel. The Excel portion of the preassessment should be structured as lesson-related. In other words, students should be provided with mini lessons on using Excel and then be given an assessment over the material. Other items might include questions about the relationship between the two variables and how they can estimate the precision of the fit of the straight line. **Ongoing assessment:** Keep a record of students' responses to the questions in small and large group: Did they understand how outliers would affect their line? Did they realize that the more the two variables are related, the more they will approximate a perfect straight line?	**Preassessment:** Those students who are able to create scatterplots, fit a straight line to the data, and use Excel (with or without the mini lessons) will enter their data into Excel and use Excel to create a scatterplot and linear model. **Ongoing assessment:** Keep a record of students' responses to the questions in small and large group: Did they understand how outliers would affect their line? Did they realize that the more the two variables are related, the more they will approximate a perfect straight line? *To evaluate the advanced learners, create a checklist on using Excel to create scatterplots and linear models.*

Subject: Math Learning Progression
Domain: Statistics and Probability (Grades 6–12)

High School Problem	Both typical and advanced learners complete the Census at School survey, which is an international classroom project and is found on the American Statistical Association website (see link in Implementation). The learners download a random sample of the survey data to conduct a statistical investigation, enter the data into Excel, and model the data using a linear regression model. Typical students investigate a research problem formulated by the teacher.	
Standard: S-ID 7		
Interpret the slope (rate of change) and the intercept (constant term) of a linear model in the context of the data.	*Advanced students formulate their own question that can be analyzed using a linear model.*	
	Typical	**Advanced**
	1. Tell the students that they will be answering a series of questions on an international survey and then using these data to conduct a statistical investigation. 2. Students work individually to complete the survey (pairing up when measurements need to be taken). 3. Tell the typical learners that a student in grade 4 wants to know if reaction time (use information from question 10 on the survey) improves though high school. With the whole group of typical learners, ask the students to suggest some questions that they would need to consider when using the *continued*	1. Tell the students that they will be answering a series of questions on an international survey and then using these data to conduct a statistical investigation. 2. Students work individually to complete the survey (pairing up when measurements need to be taken). 3. *Put the advanced learners in a group. Ask them to write several research questions using the census data that can be modeled using a linear regression model.* 4. *After the students decide on their research question, have them write a rationale describing the characteristics of a good random sample they should select from the U.S.* *continued*

High School Problem, *continued*

census to help her determine if this is the case. Possible questions include: Is the relationship between age and reaction time different for males and females? Will the results of different random samples drawn from the census be the same? How big of a random sample should they use? What ages should be included in the random sample? 4. Learners break into groups of six to eight and each group downloads a random sample based on the answers to the questions above. 5. Learners will enter the data into Excel and use Excel to create a linear model. 6. Discuss the linear models in a whole group. Ask the following questions: What is the slope of the line? What does the slope represent? What is the constant? What does the constant represent? Write the prediction equations and solve them for ages = 12, 15, 18. Were the slopes and constants the same for all groups? Why?	*Census at School data. Once the teacher approves the rationale, the learners will select a random sample using the Census at School Random Sampler tool.* 5. Learners will enter the data into Excel and use Excel to create a linear model. 6. Discuss the linear models in a whole group. Ask the following questions: What is the slope of the line? What does the slope represent? What is the constant? What does the constant represent? *Write the prediction equations and solve them for selected values of the X variable. If you collected additional random samples and rerun the analysis, would the linear model be the same for all samples? Why?*

Implementation

Based on your preassessment, put the students into homogeneous groups. Those who already know how to formulate research questions, select random samples, and create linear models would be in the advanced learners group. Go to http://www.amstat.org/censusatschool/index.cfm to download the student survey and make copies for each student in class. Explain to the students that they will work individually (pairing up when necessary) to complete the survey and then go to the Census at School website to enter their completed survey

continued

High School Problem, *continued*

data. Next, share the four components of statistical problem solving found in the *Guidelines for Assessment and Instruction* (GAISE) *Report* (Franklin, Cader, Mewborn, Moreno, Peck, & Scheaffer, 2005): formulate questions, collect data, analyze data, and interpret results. As the advanced learners are formulating their research questions and random sampling plan, tell the typical learners that they will investigate the following research question: Does reaction time improve from grade 4 through high school? In addition, tell them that they will use the Census at School Random Sampler tool to select a random sample. When all learners have selected their random sample and created their linear model in Excel, bring all learners together in a large group. Ask questions about their linear models.

For those students who need assistance with using Excel to create a linear model, download and make copies of the relevant pages (through Figure 7) of instructions from this website: http://www.ncsu.edu/chemistry/resource/excel/excel.html#cal.

Assessment	Typical	Advanced
	Preassessment: Design a preassessment that includes writing research questions that can be analyzed using a linear model, selecting random samples based on selected research questions, and using data to construct a linear model.	**Preassessment:** Those students who understand how to write research questions that can be analyzed using a linear model, how to select a random sample, and how to use data to construct a linear model will develop one or more research questions based on the Census at School survey data, draw a random sample, and construct a linear model using Excel.
	Ongoing assessment: Keep a record of students' responses to the questions in small and large group: Were the characteristics of the random sample they selected representative of the population under study? Did the students understand that the slope represents the amount of change in the *continued*	**Ongoing assessment:** Keep a record of students' responses to the questions in small and large group: Were the characteristics of *continued*

High School Problem, *continued*

dependent variable given a one-unit change in the independent variable? Did the students understand the meaning of the constant? Were they able to make predictions based on the prediction equation?	the random sample they selected representative of the population under study? Did the students understand that the slope represents the amount of change in the dependent variable given a one-unit change in the independent variable? Did the students understand the meaning of the constant? Were they able to make predictions based on the prediction equation? *To evaluate the advanced learners, create a rubric based on the four components of statistical problem solving: formulate questions, collect data, analyze data, and interpret results.*

Chapter 5

Management Strategies

In implementing learning experiences for typical, advanced, and gifted learners in mathematics, teachers need to know how to organize and manage small groups and individuals within the classroom so that individual strengths and weaknesses can be addressed. All educators need to be aware of ways of developing program services and supports within the school and the school district so that students might accelerate across grade levels and participate in extended learning opportunities.

Within-Class Instructional Management System

Teachers are able to provide content-based acceleration and enrichment for gifted and advanced students within the classroom setting. Within-class strategies may include curriculum compacting, where after pretesting, students are allowed to do alternative activities; forming small homogeneous groups; engaging in individual research projects; and using contracts or menus. To implement any of these strategies, the teacher within a classroom setting needs to establish an instructional management system so that students can work independently or in small groups. For a system to be effective, the teacher must ensure that students in the classroom know:

1. What they already know and can do and what they need to learn (e.g., the knowledge and skills within a curriculum framework or scope and sequence). In other words, are the students able to describe what they are learning and what they already know about the concepts?

2. How to find resources that are aligned to the mathematics domain. These include both human (e.g., teacher, peers, mentors) and material resources (e.g., games, web-based materials, books, manipulatives).

3. When, where, and how to use the resources. Students need to know not only what is available but also how and when to use them. For example, where might students find math manipulatives, how might they be used to solve problems, and when are they allowed to use them?

4. When, where, and how to demonstrate what they have learned. Once students have interacted with the learning resources, do they know how to show what they have learned? Will they demonstrate their knowledge on a traditional type of assessment, in a small group with the teacher, or in a project?

5. What they should do when they have demonstrated a specific degree of mastery or proficiency and then what to do next. Students need to know if they have learned the knowledge and skills at a mastery or proficiency level and if they are ready to go deeper into the standard or advance to a new standard.

To implement effective instructional management systems, the teacher needs to pay careful attention to how the room is arranged, how the materials are managed, teacher and student schedules, and teacher and student records.

Room Arrangement

The room arrangement should facilitate the learning experiences in the classroom—what is being learned by individuals and/or groups, how it is being learned or individual student preferences, and individual variations in rate or how much time is needed for problem solving or learning new concepts.

Although *whole-group instruction* is difficult in providing for individual differences in rate or preference, it may be useful at times for giving directions, providing an overview of the standards and learning experiences, asking questions, fostering discussions, or summarizing what has been learned. If the teacher wants interaction between students, then the whole-group area needs to be arranged in a way that students are able to see one another instead of in a grid arrangement. In this way, students are able to have eye contact, visibly demonstrate a problem-solving strategy that they might have used, and communicate with one another directly instead of through the teacher. For example, instead of the students responding to the teacher's questions, a student might lead the discussion, which is easier to accomplish when the class is in a circular or other type of face-to-face arrangement (e.g., parallel rows facing each other).

Small groups allow for even more student interaction than whole groups. Students face one another and work together. Although some of the interactions between students may be more controlled by the teacher (e.g., the teacher asks a question and then the students respond in small groups), others may involve more teamwork in solving an unstructured problem and last for longer periods of time. Although the teacher might vary the depth or complexity of the problems that each group solves (e.g., one group might be measuring the growth of plants, another might be posing questions about factors that contribute to the growth, and another might be creating more controlled experiments; see learning experience for grade 3), any type of grouping still limits individual variations in rate and preference. These types of variations might be addressed through the use of stations or centers.

Stations or centers might be used with students who prefer or need alternate learning experiences instead of the ones that are being used with whole or small groups, who finish their work early, or who need extended work with a particular project. Centers might vary formats or response modes to address student preferences for learning. For example, a teacher might organize the room into a variety of distinct areas or centers where students may choose different learning activities for the same math concept. Students might also establish centers for other students that display the results of projects (e.g., an experiment that showed the effects of an intervention) or create podcasts about what they have learned. These centers can also be multi-leveled so that each student might be solving a different problem to reinforce or learn new concepts that are aligned to his or her preassessment information. For example, some students might be developing bar graphs to interpret data, whereas others might be developing line-plot graphs. Centers may be placed around the room, allowing for students to have a central work area with their own individual desks or the teacher may divide the entire room into areas with each student having a separate cubby to store his or her personal items.

For a center to be effective, the students and teacher need to understand its purpose. How does it relate to what each of the students is learning or needs to learn? How does it relate to developing critical and creative thinking skills needed for investigating new problems? Centers also need to be organized so that students can use the learning experiences within the center independently, which may entail making them more self-directing and allowing for self-assessment so students receive immediate feedback regarding their work. To ensure that the materials are used appropriately, the teacher will want to establish rules for each of the centers so that the students understand when and how the materials should be used. Finally, each of the centers will require an adequate introduction, particularly at the elementary level, which may require having students role play the use of the materials within the center. In all cases, teachers need to pay attention and reinforce those students who are working independently, showing perseverance when solving problems, using appropriate tools strategically, and demonstrating other standards of mathematical practice (NGA & CCSSO, 2010a).

When arranging the classroom, the teacher will want to consider these other ideas:

- Involve the students in planning and setting up some of the centers. For example, the teacher might show the students how the problems that are on task cards are designed and aligned with specific standards, then allow students to contribute their own problems. In this way, the center is dynamic, is related to student interest, and encourages their creativity.

- Plan for large- and small-group instruction areas. Even if the teacher has divided the classroom into distinct learning areas, he or she will still want to have an area for small- and large-group instruction.

- Limit time in certain centers. Some centers that are very attractive to students, such as computers, need to be structured for sharing. Time limits may be imposed with a kitchen timer, or the number of learning experiences may be limited.

- Control the number of students in some centers. In some cases, you may want to limit the number of students by controlling the number of chairs in the center, putting the limitation in the center rules, or using a stop sign to communicate when the center is full.

- Plan for traffic flow. Pathways should be made around centers instead of through them. Centers should also be located in a variety of areas around the room so that one space does not become overly congested.

- Prepare quiet and noisy areas. Noisy areas might be placed near the door while quiet centers might be located in far corners of the room. Independent stations should also be considered for individual projects and for those students who like to work more independently and quietly.

- Create centers that might link to other areas in the school, such as the media center, an outside school garden, the playground, the hallway, and so on. For example, students might be designing a full-scale model of a much smaller object in the hallway or on the playground.

In summary, the way that a room is arranged should purposefully facilitate learning and allow for the management of a variety of groups and learning experiences—large and small groups, individual projects, games, and so on. In this way, gifted and advanced students will have opportunities to select or create tasks that match their abilities and interests. Varied learning experiences also enable students to learn the same concepts but in different ways. Organizing these learning experiences into independent centers or stations helps students organize their own learning and allows students to move from one task to another without hurrying or waiting for a new lesson to begin. In this way, students have time to persevere in problem solving and in developing other standards of mathematical practice. With increasing options, each student can assume more and more responsibility, create new areas of interest, and increase the chances that he or she will develop into an innovative mathematician (Sheffield, 2003).

Materials Management

Assume that a primary teacher receives a set of consumable math workbooks to use at the beginning of the school year. The teacher administers a pretest or some other type of formative assessment and notices that the advanced students need different workbooks at different grade levels, some students know some but not all of the concepts in the workbook, and some students do not appear to be learning from the workbook. If the teacher decides to address these differences, she or he needs to develop a system for organizing the classroom materials.

In deciding how to organize materials, the teacher needs to identify the purpose for the new organization system.

Does the teacher want to organize the materials so that they can be used more independently? In this case, the materials will need to be self-directing and perhaps allow for self-assessment depending on the task itself. To design or adapt materials that can be used independently, teachers need to identify for the students what they want them to do, what tools or materials they will use, how they will know when they are finished, and how they will know if they have been successful. Directions to guide independent learning might be included on task cards or within a center or station. Figure 5.1 illustrates what the rules in the construction center might say.

Other ways of organizing materials to be used more independently are to use symbols for nonreaders, place folders in a file box and label them according to domain and standard, put manipulatives in see-through plastic boxes, or organize games in folders, portfolios, or small boxes. Students may also be involved in self-assessment if the materials allow for small-group discussions or presentations, provide model examples, have a rubric or criteria for multiple correct answers, are aligned to a teacher's guide that the students might use, or have the answers on the back side of a puzzle or problem.

Does the teacher want to provide more choices for the students so that they can choose how they will learn the concepts or how they will demonstrate what they have learned? In this case, the teacher will want to vary the learning experiences according to response dimensions or formats. For example, with response dimensions, student-selected products or performances that require oral responses might include debates, interviews, speeches, discussions, and presentations. Those that require written responses might include essays, reports, critiques, journals, or steps used in solving a problem. Those that require visual responses might include posters, pictographs, flow charts, or scale drawings, and those that require kinesthetic responses might include models, experiments, demonstrations, and dramatizations. A student

---

Rules for Construction Center

- Develop a 1:8, 1:16, 1:32 scale plan of a house, an aircraft, a garden, or another structure of your choosing.

- Design your plan, identifying the components of the model—the rooms, the parts of the garden or airplane, etc.

- When you are finished with your design, check the scale plan and its components using the rubric at the center.

- Using your plan, construct the object using the materials in the center.

- When you have completed your object, sign up for a conference with the teacher.

Figure 5.1. Rules for construction center.

---

might be able to select from among these various ways to show his or her understanding of a concept. For example, after learning about fractions, a student might demonstrate the steps needed to transform 1/2 to 4/8 by using construction paper and scissors (kinesthetic), might develop a podcast to explain equivalent fractions to another student (oral and visual), might develop a poster that shows different equivalent fractions (visual), or might write several story problems that involve equivalent fractions (written). All of these choices might be included on a menu (see Figure 5.2) with the types and kinds of fractions varying based upon the achievement levels of different students.

Teachers might also want to vary the task formats and use games, small-group discussion, books, construction, videos, role play, computer programs, direct teaching, simulations, or manipulatives. For example, measurement choices might involve designing measurement experiments, collecting items that can be measured, demonstrating recipes using tools of measurement, building a pattern, creating a unit of measurement, writing measurement problems, and discussing new measurement systems. Varying the different response dimensions and task formats adapts to the students' preferences for learning and provides ongoing opportunities for assessments that match students' characteristics.

Equivalent Fractions Menu

After studying your fractions, select one or more of the following options to share what you have learned:

1. Transform fractions by using construction paper and scissors.

2. Develop a 5-minute podcast to explain equivalent fractions to another student.

3. Develop a poster showing different equivalent fractions.

4. Write two story problems that involve equivalent fractions.

Figure 5.2. Equivalent fractions menu.

Does the teacher want to create multi-level learning experiences so that students are doing different tasks that are related to the preassessment results? If so, then the teacher will need to align the independent tasks to specific standards that students need to learn. In aligning these tasks, the teacher first identifies the content, the process, and the product that is described in the standard. For example, the grade 3 standard states: Generate measurement data by measuring lengths using rulers marked with halves and fourths of an inch. The content in this standard is "lengths of halves and fourths of an inch," the process is "measuring with rulers," and the product is "generating measurement data." Based on preassessments, learning experiences might include introducing some of the students to the content of "halves" and the process of "measuring" in a small-group, problem-based lesson or providing a teacher-designed PowerPoint on a computer or DVD. Other students who may already know the content of "measuring to halves" might be learning about "measuring to fourths" by measuring objects in the room or specific objects at a construction center and generating data (the product) for other students to confirm or disprove. More advanced students might be "measuring to eighths and/or 16ths" or generating measurement data that they might use in a scale drawing in a construction center that includes task card problems such as the one shown in Figure 5.3.

2-D Scale Drawing

You are to draw a 2-D model of a roller coaster with the following dimensions using 11-inch x 18-inch graph paper. Your drawing should be a 1/16 scale of the model.

1. Start with an 8-inch vertical drop.

2. Then a 6 3/4-inch, 45-degree downward slope.

3. Next a 11 5/16-inch level area with a 6 1/2-inch loop in the middle of the 11 5/16-inch length.

4. Finish with a 30-degree upward slope that is 12 inches long.

Remember to include title and scale factor on your drawing. Use a ruler and other measuring devices to be precise.

Figure 5.3. Task card problem.

For all of these purposes (i.e., independent learning, student choice, and multilevel learning experiences), the teacher needs a way to catalogue all of the tasks. Teachers may decide to create a spreadsheet that shows the tasks that are aligned to each standard for easy reference. In this way, as specific tasks are field-tested, they can be added or subtracted from the list. Another purpose for cataloguing tasks is to communicate to the students the optional learning experiences that might be available to them for learning a particular standard. Older students might be able to use the same system that the teacher is keeping—examining a spreadsheet, a notebook, or a chart to find materials.

Younger children or nonreaders, on the other hand, may need to use codes. Codes may be colors, letters, numbers, symbols, and so on. For example, letters might be assigned to each of the math domains (MD for measurement and data), a color for a particular level (yellow = kindergarten; blue = first grade; red = second grade), and a symbol for a particular type of task ("star" for game, "square" for computer, "heart" for teacher, etc.). Thus, using these examples, MD with a blue star might indicate that the task was a game and related to the grade 1 measurement and data standard. Further coding might indicate a particular mathematical practice standard such as reasoning abstractly, constructing an argument, using appropriate tools, making use of structure, and so on. In Figure 5.4, the star represents first grade, MD represents measurement and data, and the questions focus the student on how he or she is interpreting the data. The young student might use this card to find the activities in each of the centers (e.g., the square indicates a workbook, the triangle indicates a game, the star indicates partner work, the heart indicates instruction in small groups, and the check indicates self-assessment). As the student completes each of the activities, he or she places a check on the line. After all of the activities are completed, the student is ready to sign up for small-group instruction or a conference with the teacher.

The major purpose for all of the systems is to help the teacher find a way to manage materials so that each student's abilities and interests match the learning resources.

Scheduling

Teachers have a variety of schedules that they use in their schools and classrooms. Those described in this section are schedules within the classroom that manage individuals, small groups, and whole-group learning experiences.

The first example, Figure 5.5, shows how a teacher has divided the class into four learning teams. This teacher revolves the teams through a series of learning experiences that relate to a math domain. Some are independent and some are teacher directed. With this type of schedule, the teacher might provide for learner differences by having different activities in different areas for homogeneously grouped teams or even for individuals within each team.

The next example, Figure 5.6, shows a block schedule where the teacher has more flexible grouping options. In this schedule, the teacher identifies times when students will work together as a whole class, when she will meet individually with students, when she will provide instruction to small groups, and when

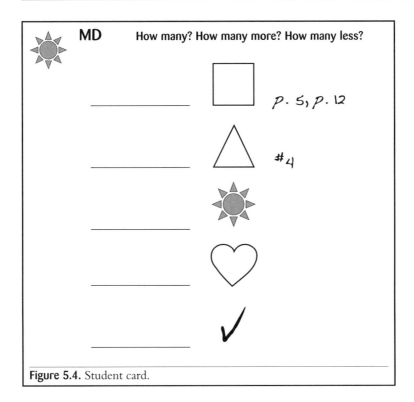

MD   How many? How many more? How many less?

p. 5, p. 12

#4

Figure 5.4. Student card.

students will share what they have learned. This schedule allows the teacher to schedule different events daily. If math activities need to be within a single period, the teacher's schedule might show events for different days during the week. For example, conferences might be on Wednesdays and progress evaluations on Thursdays.

In a classroom, both teachers and students keep schedules. Teachers will primarily keep schedules of times for instruction, individual conference, assessment and evaluation, and special events (see Figure 5.7). At the beginning of each day or period, the teacher brings the students together and explains the scheduled options with the students. At this time, the students might also add other special events that they want to share. Events may be scheduled for the day or for the week.

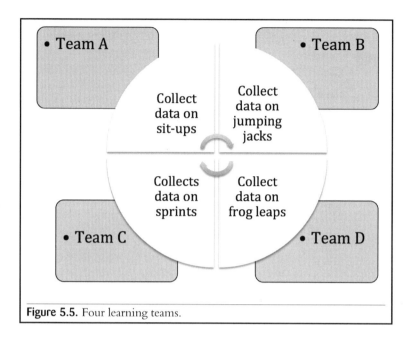

Figure 5.5. Four learning teams.

Teacher's Schedule

8:00–8:30	Plan daily events with students
8:30–9:00	Individual conferences
9:30–10:00	Direct instruction/discussion in math
11:00–12:00	Progress evaluations
1:30–2:00	Special event: Math project

Figure 5.6. Teacher's schedule.

For nonreaders and students who do not read digital clocks, times might be announced orally or by color. For example, a teacher might hold up the color "red" and those children who are in the "red" group for that day would come to the teacher while the other students work in teams or independently. The next day, the "red" group might be comprised of different students. Those in each group would be announced at the initial class meeting.

Mr. Saxon's Plans—Tuesday

Graphs Center—9:30
Tony, Maria, Lee, Juan, Trina

Using a Graphing Calculator Lesson—10:00
Anyone who is interested

Individual Conferences—at my desk from 10:30–11:30
1. Tony (bring math work)
2. Jennifer (bring project)
3. Lisa (bring book)
4.
5.
6.

Whole Group Discussion—1:00

Novel Discussion—2:00
Jeremy, Terrill, Janet, Danielle

Figure 5.7. Teacher's plans.

Students might maintain schedules of learning activities for the math period on an individual contract or in a diary (see Figure 5.8). In this diary, the student identified when she worked on the standard, the standard itself, the materials used in learning about the standard, how she measured her progress on the assessment, and other comments.

Teacher and student schedules are a way of managing the environment so that students know which learning activities to use, the order of the learning activities, the times for direct instruction, the times for individual conferences, the times for working and sharing with their peers, the length of time for completing each learning activity, the number of learning activities to do, and the time for assessment.

Record Keeping

In an instructional management system that involves not only large groups but also small groups and individual projects, records are needed for planning future learning experiences and

Rema's Math Diary				
Today's Date	Standard	Materials I Used	Progress	Comments
10/15	DM 5	Game	Partner Check	
10/16	DM 5	Workbook p. 75		Need to check problems with MariCarmen
10/17	DM 5	Small-group discussion	Passed assessments	
10/18	DM 6	PowerPoint		Not sure about fractions

Figure 5.8. Student math diary.

accountability. What have students learned? What do they need to learn? How did they demonstrate what they learned? What were the qualities of their work? Records might also be kept regarding what resources students used, when they used them, and the resources' effectiveness.

When students are doing multiple activities at the same time, most teachers find it easier to share the responsibility of record keeping. Students will assume greater responsibility for keeping records of what they are learning, the resources they used, when they used them, and how well they performed on each of the tasks. The teacher assumes the major responsibility for keeping records of how the student demonstrated what he or she had learned, the quality of his or her work, and the need for more monitoring, instruction, enrichment, and/or acceleration. Based on records, the teacher can schedule large-group instruction with the entire class, small-group instruction with particular students, and individual conferences for assessing progress, planning extensions, or advancing the student to new standards.

Class record forms. Figure 5.9 shows a way of keeping a class record. Notice that the teacher has added the content of the standard in the columns and the names of the students in the

Class Record Form

Name	Comments	Gather Data	Graph Results	Interpret	Pose Questions
Aaron		X	X		
Alex		X	X		
Alicia		X	X		
Anne		X	X		
Angelo		X			
Brittany		X			
Candice		X	X		
Danielle		X	X		
David		X			
DJ	Compare data	X	X		
Emma		X	X		
Eric		X	X		
Haley	More practice with <, >	X	X		
Karen	Compare data	X	X		
Kim		X	X		
Mario	Next standard	X	X		X
Michelle		X	X		
Rashid	Next standard	X	X		X
Robin	More practice with <, >	X	X		
Stephanie		X	X		
Tom	Next standard	X	X		X
Vanessa	More practice with <, >	X	X		

Figure 5.9. Class record form.

rows. This form helps the teacher know which students have learned to gather data, graph results, interpret results, use a bar graph, and pose questions that require a quantitative response (see Grade 1 Problem in Sample Activities, pp. 55–57). As you will notice, Mario, Rashid, and Tom know how to pose questions and are ready for a new standard; Karen and DJ still require instruction about comparing data; and Brittany, David, and Angelo need assistance with graphing. The teacher will be able to use this form to schedule small-group instruction time and prepare Mario, Rashid, and Tom for the next standard.

Individual teacher record forms. Teachers might also want to keep more qualitative information about students on a notebook computer, notepad, or in a loose-leaf notebook. These notes might include information about when the teacher met with a particular student in small-group or individual conferences, the student's progress, and activities that appear to be effective with this particular student. In the example in Figure 5.10, the teacher noted that on October 27 during a math conference, Sandra discussed the naming of fractional parts, ordered them on a number line, and was ready for equivalent fractions. She also indicated the types and kinds of resources that Sandra had been using to learn the information and noted which ones were effective with her.

Students and teachers might also contribute examples of the students' math work in an expandable file of portfolio items or in a web-based e-folio system. Both students and teachers could reflect on the student's understanding of content, process, or products. The e-folio might follow the student from one grade level to the next and provide information to teachers about the student's abilities and interests.

Individual student record forms. For the student, record keeping provides a means for developing responsibility for his or her own learning and supports a feeling of accomplishment. Students need to be aware of what is being learned, the purpose of the activity, and their progress. Students may keep a record of activities that they have completed. The example of the growth chart in Figure

Name: Sandra Gustafson			
Standard/ Objective	**Activities**	**Assessment**	**Comments**
Standard 3.NF.2b Understand fraction as a number on a number line, represent fractions on a number line.	Small-group discussion, game, task cards with number line activities.	10/20—small group; 10/27— conference.	Can order fractions on a number line with denominators up to eighths.

Figure 5.10. Record of qualitative information during individual conferences.

5.11 describes each of the record form characteristics—name of the objective, activities, and progress.

To use this growth chart, the teacher would initially administer a pretest to the class of students. The teacher would then indicate on the student's growth chart which specific objectives the student needed to learn. Depending on the student, the teacher might indicate the resources that she would like the student to use, or she might leave it open to the student to select the resources. After the student has successfully completed the indicated tasks, he or she will take an assessment at a set time or sign up for a conference with the teacher. In the example, the student knew how to make line-plots, use fractions, and interpret these types of data. He did not appear to have reached proficiency on the other objectives. The teacher decided that she wanted the student to think more deeply about the data and suggested that he solve problems using line-plot data. She indicated that she wanted the student to use the problem cards and the book, and then participate in a small-group discussion with the teacher on Friday.

Other excellent student record forms that teachers might consider using include activity logs, bar graphs of progress, curriculum compactors, and learning contracts (see Adams & Pierce, 2012; Reis, Burns, & Renzulli, 1992; Tomlinson & Imbeau,

Student Growth Chart

Name: _____   Dates: _____

Objective	Assessment		Teacher	Book	Computer	Games	Problem Cards
	Pre–	Post–					
1. Make line–plot to display data.	✗	✗					
2. Use fractions to display data.	✗	✗					
3. Use decimals to display data.							
4a. Interpret data.	✗	✗	✓	✓		✓	✓
4b. Interpret data using measures of central tendency.							
5. Solve problems using data.			✔ Friday	✓			✓
6. Make predictions using data.							
7. Independent research.							

Figure 5.11. Student growth chart.

2010; Winebrenner, 2001). These forms are also based on information acquired through assessment.

Program Services and Supports Within the School Building

A variety of program services and supports can be provided within the school so that gifted and advanced students in math experience conceptually challenging and complex content (NAGC, 2010). Approaches may involve cross-grade-level teaming, moving students across grade levels, classroom schedule changes, or using resources outside of the school.

Teachers will need to work together to implement a variety of acceleration and enrichment options. For example, if a student accelerates within a classroom at a particular grade level, this acceleration will affect the curriculum in subsequent grade levels. Teachers will want to develop a flexible scope and sequence that allows students to move with their peers from grade to grade in a seamless situation, while at the same time learning new concepts in mathematics. In some cases, particularly with students who may be advanced in mathematics by two or more grade levels, teachers may want to provide single-subject acceleration where a student goes to an above-level classroom to participate in math activities that are designed to challenge the student and provide the depth necessary for encouraging problem solving and creativity. At the secondary level, teachers may want to create separate sections for students who are advanced so that they have more opportunities to delve more deeply into complex problems. In small schools, gifted and advanced students in mathematics might also benefit from cross-grade projects where students with particular interests might work together on a math project, such as implementing schoolwide interventions (see Grade 4 Problem in Sample Activities, pp. 66–71) or planning a schoolwide garden with information gleaned from classroom research (see Grade 3 Problem in Sample Activities, pp. 62–65).

Some strategies might also require schedule changes. For example, one of the best-known between-class grouping plans is the Joplin Plan, wherein students go to different classrooms to receive instruction geared toward their readiness level (Floyd, 1954; Kulik, 1992). In this plan, all of the teachers teach math at a particular time period. At the conclusion of the time, students return to their regular classroom setting. Researchers have reported that this plan produces substantial academic gains (Kulik, 1992, 2003; Rogers, 1991, 2002).

Another approach for students who are particularly advanced in mathematics but desire to remain with their peers is distance learning. For example, elementary or middle school students might access an advanced course at the high school or even university level. A student might go to the library or media center and "attend" an algebra, statistics, precalculus, or calculus course that best meets his or her needs and readiness level.

Other supports might be provided on- or off-campus by mentors, who specialize in a student's area of interest. For example, a group of high school students who were passionate about astronomy established an afterschool club and were guided by an astronomy professor at a local university. The principal provided an empty classroom, which the students eventually filled with all types of equipment and resources. They used every inch of the available chalkboards to write formulas and models.

Finally, competitions in mathematics can be stimulating to some of the students and provide more opportunities to interact with their peers and engage them in solving more complex problems. These competitions may be found in Appendix C.

Program Services and Supports Within the School District and With Partners

In all cases, the school district will need to be involved in supporting services to students who are gifted and advanced in mathematics. Just as in an individual school, it may be helpful to examine the school district's overall scope and sequence in math to determine if it is sufficiently flexible in providing for students' readiness to learn new concepts or participate in advanced math courses. The district will want to include options for grade or course skipping, which may entail the development of end-of-course or end-of-grade exams or other diagnostic tools to determine student placement needs. In these cases, policies will be needed for whole-grade acceleration, where a student might skip a grade; grade telescoping, where two grades of curriculum are completed within a single year; and early entrance options—to kindergarten or to college (IRPA, NAGC, & CSDPG, 2009).

Moreover, elementary or middle school students may need transportation to another building to attend a more advanced course in mathematics, or a high school teacher may need to provide instruction to a group of middle school students. Teachers will also need training to provide advanced courses that offer college-level coursework for students as early as middle school.

The school district will also want to establish partnerships with colleges and universities. In this way, advanced students may enroll in dual credit courses that provide not only credits toward higher education degrees but also options that might not otherwise be supported by the school district's resources (e.g., specialized courses or instructors).

Summary

The delivery of program services and supports that challenge every learner involves teachers, principals, and other school district administrators. Teachers need to learn how to develop content-based acceleration and enrichment for gifted and advanced students within the classroom. Strategies may include curriculum compacting, forming homogeneous groups, engaging in individual research projects, and using contracts or menus. Implementing these strategies requires an instructional management system that pays attention to room arrangement, how the materials are managed, teacher and student schedules, and teacher and student records. Administrators must become involved as students accelerate across grade levels or schools so that students progress seamlessly. Some of these strategies will require within-school schedule changes or across-the-district policy changes. These policies need to address whole-grade acceleration, grade telescoping, early entrance options, and transportation, among other issues. In all cases, flexibility is key in implementing the Common Core State Standards for Mathematics that is differentiated for typical, advanced, and gifted learners.

Conclusion

Gifted and advanced students in mathematics deserve to have a curriculum that addresses their strengths and increases their passion for mathematics. No single curriculum, set of learning experiences, or standards is adequate for addressing these learners' variations in abilities, interests, rates of learning, and responsiveness to educational interventions. We want to emphasize these important concepts from this book in our concluding comments.

1. Although the CCSSM emphasize thinking, problem solving, collaboration, and communication, they are not sufficiently advanced to accommodate the needs of learners who are gifted in mathematics.

2. The Standards of Mathematical Practice are important process skills that all students need to develop, but an additional standard is needed that emphasizes creativity to encourage the development of innovative mathematicians among students gifted and advanced in mathematics.

3. No scope and sequence or learning progression is appropriate for every student. The progressions need to be modified by attending to the learning rate and achievement level of the students.

4. Vertical and lateral alignments of standards and clusters of standards within the CCSSM provide avenues for accelerating and enriching the mathematics learning experiences of gifted and advanced students.

5. Aptitude, as well as achievement in mathematics, needs to be used in recognizing early talent in mathematics. Early identification is critical so that curriculum and programming can be adjusted.

6. With appropriate interventions, the learning trajectories of gifted and advanced students in mathematics may be accelerated, allowing them to reach college-level courses by their junior or senior year in high school.

7. Some gifted students in mathematics may need radical acceleration, not just modification or differentiation of the learning progression.

8. Along with acceleration, gifted and advanced students need to continue to develop their passion for mathematics. Participation in advanced coursework as well as math clubs, apprenticeships, and competitions helps students intensify their motivation for mathematics.

9. Learning experiences need to be differentiated. Some of these strategies may include accelerated pacing, depth and complexity, creativity, interdisciplinary connections, concept-based or thematic curriculum, and higher order thinking.

10. Use of formative assessments that include off-level testing and complex problem solving are critical in monitoring progress and in determining which students are ready for above-level content.

11. Teachers need to know how to manage a variety of activities to allow for acceleration and enrichment of gifted and advanced students in mathematics.

Teachers are key in developing students' interest in mathematics and differentiating the curriculum. Their deep understanding of the mathematics domain, mathematical practices, and creativity will enable them to encourage their students in becoming innovative mathematicians. How teachers are prepared and supported in the classroom is therefore much more important than a standards-based curriculum. Teachers need the knowledge, skills, and tools to implement a curriculum that is successful with advanced and gifted learners in mathematics.

References

Adams, C. M., & Pierce, R. L. (2012). *Differentiation that really works—Math: Grades 6–12*. Waco, TX: Prufrock Press.

Adelman, C. (1999). *Answers in the toolbox*. Retrieved from http://www2ed.gov/pubs/Toolbox/index.html

Assouline, S. G., & Lupkowski-Shoplik, A. E. (2011). *Developing math talent: A comprehensive guide to math education for gifted students in elementary and middle school* (2nd ed.). Waco, TX: Prufrock Press.

Barbeau, E., & Taylor, P. J. (Eds.). (2009). *Challenging mathematics in and beyond the classroom: The 16th ICMI study*. New York, NY: Springer.

Betts, G. T., & Kercher, J. K. (1999). *Autonomous learner model: Optimizing ability*. Greely, CO: Autonomous Learning.

Bressoud, D. M. (2009). Is the sky still falling? *Notices of the AMS, 56,* 20–25.

Chamberlin, S. (2010). Mathematical problems that optimize learning for academically advanced students in grades K–6. *Journal of Advanced Academics, 22,* 52–76.

Chapin, S. H., O'Connor, C., & Anderson, N. C. (2009). *Classroom discussions: Using math talk to help students learn.* Sausalito, CA: Math Solutions.

Colangelo, N., Assouline, S. G., & Gross, M. U. M. (Eds.). (2004). *A nation deceived: How schools hold back America's brightest students* (Vol. 2). Iowa City: University of Iowa, The Connie Belin & Jacqueline N. Blank International Center for Gifted Education and Talent Development.

Coleman, M. R., & Johnsen, S. K. (Eds.). (2013). *Implementing RtI with gifted students: Service models, trends, and issues.* Waco, TX: Prufrock Press.

College Board. (2009). *AP Examination volume changes (1999– 2009).* New York, NY: College Board. Retrieved from http://professionals.collegeboard.com/profdownload/exam-volume-change-09.pdf

Common Core State Standards Writing Team. (2011). *Draft K–5 progression on measurement and data.* Tucson: University of Arizona Institute for Mathematics and Education. Retrieved from http://ime.math.arizona.edu/progressions/

Consortium for Policy Research in Education. (2011). *Learning trajectories in mathematics: A foundation for standards, curriculum, assessment, and instruction.* Retrieved from http://www.cpre. org/images/stories/cpre_pdfs/learning%20trajectories%20 in%20math_ccii%20report.pdf

Feldhusen, J. F., & Kolloff, P. B. (1986). The Purdue Three-Stage Enrichment Model at the elementary level. In J. S. Renzulli (Ed.), *Systems and models for developing programs for the gifted and talented* (pp. 126–152). Waco, TX: Prufrock Press.

Floyd, C. (1954). Meeting children's reading needs. *Elementary School Journal, 55,* 93–103.

Gavin, M. K., Casa, T. M., Adelson, J. L., Carroll, S. R., & Sheffield, L. J. (2009). The impact of advanced curriculum on the achievement of mathematically promising elementary students. *Gifted Child Quarterly, 53,* 188–202.

Hess, K. K. (2008). *Developing and using learning progressions as a schema for measuring progress.* Retrieved from http://www.nciea. org/publications/CCSSO2_KH08.pdf

Hess, K. K., & Kearns, J. (2011). *Learning progressions frame-works designed for use with the Common Core State Standards in*

Mathematics K–12. Retrieved from http://www.nciea.org/publications/Math_LPF_KH11.pdf

Illustrated Mathematics. (n.d.) *2.MD. The longest walk.* Retrieved from http://www.illustrativemathematics.org/illustrations/486

Institute for Mathematics and Education. (2012). *Progressions documents for the common core math standards.* Retrieved from http://ime.math.arizona.edu/progressions/

Institute for Research and Policy on Acceleration, National Association for Gifted Children, & Council of State Directors of Programs for the Gifted. (2009). *Guidelines for developing an academic acceleration policy.* Retrieved from http://www.accelerationinstitute.org/resources/policy_guidelines/

Johnsen, S. K. (Ed.). (2011). *Identifying gifted students: A practical guide* (2nd ed.). Waco, TX: Prufrock Press.

Johnsen, S. K., & Sheffield, L. J. (Eds.). (2013). *Using the Common Core State Standards for Mathematics with gifted and advanced learners.* Waco, TX: Prufrock Press.

Johnsen, S. K., Sulak, T., & Rollins, K. (2012). *Serving gifted students within an RtI framework.* Waco, TX: Prufrock Press.

Kaplan, S. N. (2009). Layering differentiated curricula for the gifted and talented. In F. A. Karnes & S. M. Bean (Eds.), *Methods and materials for teaching the gifted* (3rd ed., pp. 107–135). Waco, TX: Prufrock Press.

Kolitch, E. R., & Brody, L. E. (1992). Mathematics acceleration of highly talented students: An evaluation. *Gifted Child Quarterly, 36,* 78–86.

Kulik, J. A. (1992). *An analysis of the research on ability grouping: Historical and contemporary perspectives.* Storrs: University of Connecticut, National Research Center on the Gifted and Talented.

Kulik, J. A. (2003). Grouping and tracking. In N. Colangelo & G. Davis (Eds.), *Handbook of gifted education* (3rd. ed., pp. 268–81). Boston, MA: Allyn & Bacon.

Kulik, J. A. (2004). Meta-analysis studies of acceleration. In N. Colangelo, S. G. Assouline, & M. U. M. Gross (Eds.), *A nation deceived: How schools hold back America's brightest students* (Vol. II, pp. 13–22). Iowa City: University of Iowa, The Connie Belin & Jacqueline N. Blank International Center for Gifted Education and Talent Development.

Kulik, J. A., & Kulik, C-L. C. (1982). Effects of ability grouping on secondary school students: A meta-analysis. *American Educational Research Journal, 19,* 415–428.

Kulik, J. A., & Kulik, C-L. C. (1984). Effects of accelerated instruction on students. *Review of Educational Research, 54,* 409–425.

Lesh, R., Hoover, M., Hole, B., Kelly, A., & Post, T. (2000). Principles for developing thought-revealing activities for students and teachers. In R. Lesh & A. Kelly (Eds.), *Handbook of research design in mathematics and science education* (pp. 591–646). Hillsdale, NJ: Lawrence Erlbaum.

Lohman, D. F. (2011). *The Cognitive Abilities Test* (Form 7). Rolling Meadows, IL: Riverside Publishing.

Lupkowski, A. E., Assouline, S. G., & Stanley, J. C. (1990). Beyond testing: Applying a mentor model for young mathematically talented students in math. *Gifted Child Today, 67,* 2–14.

Lupkowski-Shoplik, A., Benbow, C. P., Assouline, S. G., & Brody, L. E. (2003). Talent searches: Meeting the needs of academically talented youth. In N. Colangelo & G. A. Davis (Eds.), *Handbook of gifted education* (3rd ed., pp. 204–218). Boston, MA: Allyn & Bacon.

National Assessment of Educational Progress. (2011). *NAEP mathematics framework.* Retrieved from http://nces.ed.gov/nationsreportcard/mathematics/whatmeasure.asp

National Association for Gifted Children. (2010). *NAGC Pre-K–Grade 12 Gifted Programming Standards.* Retrieved from http://www.nagc.org/ProgrammingStandards.aspx

National Association for Gifted Children, & Council for Exceptional Children, The Association for the Gifted. (2006). *NAGC-CEC teacher knowledge and skill standards for gifted and talented education*. Retrieved from http://www.nagc.org/NCATEStandards.aspx

National Center for Education Statistics. (2007). *Trends in International Mathematics and Science Study*. Retrieved from http://nces.ed.gov/timss

National Council of Teachers of Mathematics. (2008). *Random drawwing tool—Sampling distribution*. Retrieved from http://illuminations.nctm.org/ActivityDetal.aspx?ID=159

National Governors Association Center for Best Practices, & Council of Chief State School Officers. (2010a). *Common Core State Standards for Mathematics*. Retrieved from http://www.corestandards.org/the-standards

National Governors Association Center for Best Practices (NGA), & Council of Chief State School Officers. (2010b). *Common Core State Standards for Mathematics Appendix A: Designing high school mathematics courses based on the Common Core State Standards*. Retrieved from http://www.corestandards.org/assets/CCSSI_Mathematics_Appendix_A.pdf

National Governors Association Center for Best Practices, & Council of Chief State School Officers. (2010c). *Frequently asked questions*. Retrieved from http://www.corestandards.org/resources/frequently-asked-questions

Olszewski-Kubilius, P. (2004). Talent searches and accelerated programming for gifted students. In N. Colangelo, S. G. Assouline, & M. U. M. Gross (Eds.), *A nation deceived: How schools hold back America's brightest students* (Vol. II, pp.69–76). Iowa City: University of Iowa, The Connie Belin & Jacqueline N. Blank International Center for Gifted Education and Talent Development.

Partnership for 21st Century Skills. (n.d.). *Framework for 21st century learning*. Retrieved from http://www.p21.org/overview

Paul, R., & Linda, L. (2008). *The elements of reasoning and the intellectual standards*. Retrieved from http://criticalthinking.org

Reis, S. M., Burns, D. E., & Renzulli, J. S. (1992). *Curriculum compacting: The complete guide to modifying the regular curriculum for high ability students*. Waco, TX: Prufrock Press.

Renzulli, J. S. (1977). *The enrichment triad model: A guide for developing defensible programs for the gifted and talented.* Waco, TX: Prufrock Press.

Robins, J. H., & Jolly, J. L. (2011). Technical information regarding assessment. In S. K. Johnsen (Ed.), *Identifying gifted students: A practical guide* (2nd ed., pp. 75–118). Waco, TX: Prufrock Press.

Rogers, K. B. (1991). *The relationship of grouping practices to the education of the gifted and talented learner* (Report #9102). Storrs: University of Connecticut, National Research Center on the Gifted and Talented.

Rogers, K. B. (2002). *Re-forming gifted education.* Scottsdale, AZ: Great Potential Press.

Rogers, K. B. (2007). Lessons learned about educating the gifted and talented: A synthesis of the research on educational practice. *Gifted Child Quarterly, 51,* 382–396.

Rusczyk. R. (2010). Extracurricular opportunities of mathematically gifted middle school students. In M. Saul, S. G. Assouline, & L. E. Sheffield (Eds.), *The peak in the middle* (pp. 93–114). Reston, VA: National Council of Teachers of Mathematics.

Ryser, G. R. (2011). Qualitative and quantitative approaches to assessment. In S. K. Johnsen (Ed.), *Identifying gifted students: A practical guide* (2nd ed., pp. 37–61). Waco, TX: Prufrock Press.

Sarama, J., & Clements, D. H. (2009). *Early childhood mathematics education research: Learning trajectories for young children.* New York, NY: Routledge.

Saul, M., Assouline, S. G., & Sheffield, L. J. (Eds.). (2010). *The peak in the middle: Developing mathematically gifted students in the middle grades.* Reston, VA: National Council of Teachers of Mathematics.

Sheffield, L. J. (2000). Creating and developing promising young mathematicians. *Teaching Children Mathematics, 6,* 416–419.

Sheffield, L. J. (2003). *Extending the challenge in mathematics: Developing mathematical promise in K–8 students.* Thousand Oaks, CA: Corwin Press.

Sheffield, L. J. (2006). Developing mathematical promise and creativity. *Journal of the Korea Society of Mathematical Education Series D: Research in Mathematical Education, 10,* 1–11.

Silver, E. A., & Cai, J. (1996). An analysis of arithmetic problem posing by middle school students. *Journal for Research in Mathematics Education, 27,* 521–539.

Stanley, J. C. (2005). A quiet revolution: Finding boys and girls who reason exceptionally well mathematically and/or verbally and helping them get the supplemental educational opportunities they need. *High Ability Studies, 16,* 5–14.

Teague, D., Avineri, T., Belledin, C., Graves, J., Noble, R., Hernandez, M., & Robinson, D. (2011). Issues of equity for advanced students. In M. Strutchens & J. R. Quander (Eds.), *Focus in high school mathematics: Fostering reasoning and sense making for all students* (pp. 65–84). Reston, VA: National Council of Teachers of Mathematics.

Tomlinson, C. A., & Imbeau, M. B. (2010). *Leading and managing a differentiated classroom.* Alexandria, VA: Association for Supervision and Curriculum Development.

VanTassel-Baska, J. (Ed.). (2004). *Curriculum for gifted and talented students.* Thousand Oaks, CA: Corwin Press.

VanTassel-Baska, J. (Ed.). (2013). *Using the common core standards for English language arts with gifted and advanced learners.* Waco, TX: Prufrock Press.

Vaughn, V. L. (1990, November). *Meta-analysis of pull-out programs in gifted education.* Paper presented at the annual convention of the National Association for Gifted Children, Little Rock, AR.

Winebrenner, S. (2001). *Teaching gifted kids in the regular classroom: Strategies and techniques every teacher can use to meet the academic needs of the gifted and talented.* Minneapolis, MN: Free Spirit.

Wyatt, W. J., & Wiley, A. (2010). *The development of an index of academic rigor for the SAT* (College Board Research Report). New York, NY: College Board.

Appendix A

Definitions of Key Terms

Above-level testing occurs when a student is assessed with a version of a test intended for older students or students who are in grade levels above the assessed student's current grade level. This testing compensates for the fact that many tests (particularly achievement tests) have ceiling effects. In other words, there are not enough difficult items on the test. Tests that are grade-calibrated are usually too easy for gifted students and above-level testing allows educators to test a student's limits or to measure adequately the extent of the gifted student's knowledge.

Acceleration is a broad term used to describe ways in which gifted learners progress at rates faster or ages younger than typical peers. There are multiple forms and types of acceleration. The term may refer to content acceleration through preassessment, compacting, and reorganizing curriculum by unit or year, or it may refer to grade-based acceleration through whole-grade skipping, telescoping 2 years into one, or dual enrollment in middle school, high school, and college or university. It also includes more personalized approaches such as tutorials, mentorships, and independent research that also would be sensitive to the advanced starting level of these learners for instruction. Both

Advanced Placement (AP) and International Baccalaureate at the high school level represent programs of study already accelerated in content. AP courses also may be taken on a fast-track schedule earlier as appropriate.

Appropriate pacing refers to the rate at which material is taught to advanced learners. Because they are often capable of mastering new material more rapidly than typical learners, appropriate pacing would involve careful preassessment to determine readiness for more advanced material to ensure that advanced learners are not bored with the material and are being adequately challenged. Note that although students might advance quickly through some material, they should also be given time to delve more deeply into topics of interest at appropriately advanced levels of complexity and innovation.

Assessment is the way to determine the scope and degree of learning that has been mastered by the student and also to indicate the learner's readiness for new material. For purposes of gifted education, the assessments must be matched to differentiated outcomes, requiring the use of authentic approaches like performance-based and portfolio-based assessment demands. Some assessments are already constructed and available for use, exhibiting strong technical adequacy and employed in research studies while others may be teacher-developed, with opportunities to establish interrater reliability among teachers who may be using them in schools. Care should be taken to use assessments such as above-grade-level assessments that do not restrict the level of proficiency that students can demonstrate and that allow for innovative and more complex responses.

Characteristics and needs of gifted learners is the basis for differentiating any curriculum area. Mathematically talented learners often have a strong number and computation sense, see relationships, recognize patterns, make generalizations, and may be highly fluent, flexible, and original at solving problems at an earlier stage of development than typical learners. Because of this advanced readiness, these students may need to be accelerated through the basic material in mathematics in order to focus on higher level math concepts and problems.

Complexity refers to a feature of differentiation that provides advanced learners more variables to study, asks them to use multiple resources to solve a problem, or requires them to use multiple higher order skills simultaneously. The degree of complexity may depend on the developmental level of the learner, the nature of the learning task, and the readiness to take on the level of challenge required.

Creativity and innovation are used to suggest that activities used with the gifted employ opportunities for more open-ended project work that mirrors real-world professional work in solving problems in the disciplines. The terms also suggest that advanced learners are proficient in the skills and habits of mind associated with being a creator or innovator in a chosen field of endeavor. Thus, creative thinking and problem-solving skills would be emphasized.

Curriculum is a set of planned learning experiences, delineated from a framework of expectations at the goal or outcome level that represent important knowledge, skills, and concepts to be learned. Differentiated curriculum units of study already have been designed and tested for effectiveness in mathematics, or units may be developed by teachers to use in gifted instruction.

Diagnostic Testing—Prescriptive Instruction Model was developed by Julian C. Stanley at The Johns Hopkins University. The model was designed to match the level and pace of mathematics instruction to students' abilities. The student first takes an above-level mathematics aptitude test and then is administered a diagnostic mathematics achievement test. The student's instructor works with the student to ensure mastery of the concepts and skills missed on the diagnostic mathematics achievement test. In the final step, the student takes a posttest to demonstrate mastery.

Differentiation of curriculum for gifted learners is the process of adapting and modifying curriculum structures to address these characteristics and needs more optimally. Thus, curriculum goals, outcomes, and activities may be tailored for gifted learners to accommodate their needs. Typically, this process involves the use of the strategies of acceleration, complexity, depth, and creativity in combination.

Instruction is the delivery system for teaching that comprises the deliberate use of models, strategies, and supportive management techniques. For gifted learners, inquiry strategies such as problem-based learning, creative problem solving, problem posing, and critical thinking models such as Paul's reasoning model (Paul & Elder, 2008) used in independent research or within a flexible grouping approach in the regular classroom constitute instructional differentiation.

Learning progressions and scopes and sequences are designed to help teachers identify what is expected from their students and the key points along paths that indicate growth in a student's knowledge and skills. As such, they articulate the essential core concepts and processes in each mathematics domain within and across grade levels.

Rigor and relevance suggest that the curriculum experiences planned for advanced learners be sufficiently challenging yet provided in real-world or curricular contexts that matter to learners at their particular stage of development.

Talent search models seek to identify students who perform well above their age level in mathematics (or verbal areas) and provide academically challenging programs to these students. These models use above-level testing to identify these students. Students with high scores on above-level tests are provided opportunities to learn advanced materials in an accelerated learning environment.

Talent trajectory is used to describe the school span development of advanced learners in their area of greatest aptitude from K–16. It is linked to developmental stages from early childhood through adolescence and defines key interventions that aid in the talent development process specific to the subject area and desired career path.

Teacher quality refers to the movement at all levels of education to improve the knowledge base and skills of classroom teachers at Pre-K–12 levels, which is necessary for effective instruction for advanced students. It is the basis for a redesign of teacher education standards and a rationale for examining Pre-K–12 student outcomes in judging the efficacy of higher education programs for teachers. Policy makers are committed to this issue in improving our Pre-K–16 education programs.

Appendix B

Critical Readings

Assouline, S. G., & Lupkowski-Shoplik, A. (2011). *Developing math talent: A comprehensive guide to math education for gifted students in elementary and middle school* (2nd ed.). Waco, TX: Prufrock Press.

Abstract: This book is a comprehensive parent and teacher guide for developing math talent among advanced learners. This book offers a comprehensive approach to mathematics education for gifted students of elementary or middle school age. The authors provide concrete suggestions for identifying mathematically talented students, tools for instructional planning, and specific programming approaches. *Developing Math Talent* features topics such as strategies for identifying mathematically gifted learners, strategies for advocating for gifted children with math talent, how to design a systematic math education program for gifted students, specific curricula and materials that support success, and teaching strategies and approaches that encourage and challenge gifted learners. The book also includes an extensive listing of both print and Internet resources that support math education for talented children.

Barbeau, E., & Taylor, P. J. (Eds.). (2009). *Challenging mathematics in and beyond the classroom: The 16th ICMI Study*. New York, NY: Springer.

Abstract: The last two decades have seen significant innovation both in classroom teaching and in the public presentation of mathematics. Much of this development has centered on the use of games, puzzles, and investigations designed to capture interest, challenge the intellect, and encourage a more robust understanding of mathematical ideas and processes. ICMI Study 16 was commissioned to review these developments and describe experiences around the globe in different contexts, systematize the area, examine the effectiveness of the use of challenges, and set the stage for future study and development. A prestigious group of international researchers contributed to this effort. The book deals with challenges for both gifted and regular students and with building public interest in appreciation of mathematics.

Brody, L. (2004). *Grouping and acceleration practices in gifted education*. Thousand Oaks, CA: Corwin Press.

Abstract: This volume of seminal articles on grouping and acceleration from *Gifted Child Quarterly* emphasizes the importance of flexibility when assigning students to instructional groups and modifying the groups when necessary. Grouping and acceleration have proven to be viable tools to differentiate content for students with different learning needs based on cognitive abilities and achievement levels.

Chamberlin, S. A. (2006). Secondary mathematics for high-ability students. In F. A. Dixon & S. M. Moon (Eds.), *The handbook of secondary gifted education* (pp. 461–467). Waco, TX: Prufrock Press.

Abstract: This chapter offers an in-depth, research-based look at ways schools and classrooms can support the development of gifted adolescents. This author defines mathematical giftedness, provides a theoretical rationale for teaching mathematics to gifted adolescents, and describes teaching strategies and challenging curricula. Additionally, a sample plan of study for gifted math students is included.

Chamberlin, S. A. (2012). *Serving the needs of intellectually advanced mathematics students K–6*. Marion, IL: Pieces of Learning.

Abstract: Chamberlin presents a discussion about how advanced mathematics students think mathematically and steps that can be taken to develop their mathematics skills and talent. Topics incorporated in this research-based book include cognitive characteristics, identification techniques, mathematical problem solving, and more. The material in the book is consistent with the expectations outlined in both the *Principles and Standards for School Mathematics* and the *Common Core State Standards*.

Colangelo, N., Assouline, S. G., & Gross, M. U. M. (Eds.). (2004). *A nation deceived: How schools hold back America's brightest students* (Vol. 2). Iowa City: University of Iowa, The Connie Belin & Jacqueline N. Blank International Center for Gifted Education and Talent Development. (Available at http://www.accelerationinstitute.org/Nation_Deceived/Get_Report.aspx)

Abstract: Volume 2 of the two-volume international report on academic acceleration presents 11 chapters that served as the basis for Volume 1, which has been translated into 11 languages. Interviewed years later, an overwhelming majority of accelerated students say that acceleration was an excellent experience for them and that they wish they had accelerated sooner and had more accelerated experiences. They feel academically challenged and socially accepted, and they do not fall prey to the boredom that plagues many highly capable students who are forced to follow the curriculum for their age-peers. In spite of rich research evidence, schools, parents, and teachers have not accepted the idea of acceleration. *A Nation Deceived* (both volumes) presents the reasons that schools hold back America's brightest kids and shows that these reasons are simply not supported by research.

Gavin, M. K., & Adelson, J. L. (2014). Mathematics gifted education. In J. Plucker & C. M. Callahan (Eds.), *Critical issues
and practices in gifted education: What the research says* (2nd ed.
pp. 387–412). Waco, TX: Prufrock Press.
Abstract: This reference book is useful for those searching for a
summary and evaluation of the literature on giftedness and gifted
education. The book presents 53 summaries of important topics
in the field, providing relevant research and a guide to how the
research applies to gifted education. Among others, the summary
of mathematics gifted education discusses the following topics:
definition of mathematical giftedness, identification of students
who are mathematically gifted, programming options, instructional approaches, and research-based curricula approaches.

Gavin, M. K., Casa, T., Adelson, J. L., Carroll, S. R., & Sheffield,
L. J. (2009). The impact of advanced curriculum on the
achievement of mathematically promising students. *Gifted
Child Quarterly, 53,* 188–202.
Abstract: This article describes the development of Project M³:
Mentoring Mathematical Minds and reports on mathematics
achievement results for students in grades 3–5 from 11 urban and
suburban schools after exposure to the curriculum. Data analyses
indicate statistically significant differences favoring each of the
experimental groups over the comparison group on the *Iowa Test
of Basic Skills Concepts* and *Estimation Test* and on open-response
assessments at all three grade levels.

Gavin, M. K., Casa, T. M., Adelson, J. L., Carroll, S. R.,
Sheffield, L. J., & Spinelli, A. M. (2007). Project M³:
Mentoring Mathematical Minds—A research-based cur-
riculum for talented elementary students. *Journal of Advanced
Academics, 18,* 566–585.
Abstract: Project M³: Mentoring Mathematical Minds is a 5-year
Javits research grant project designed to create curriculum units
with essential elements for talented elementary students. These
units combine the exemplary teaching practice of gifted edu-

cation with the content and process standards promoted by the National Council of Teachers of Mathematics. The content at each level is at least one to two grade levels above the regular curriculum and includes number and operations, algebra, geometry and measurement, and data analysis and probability. Research was conducted on the implementation of 12 units in 11 different schools—nine in Connecticut and two in Kentucky. The sample consisted of approximately 200 mathematically talented students entering third grade, with most remaining in the project through fifth grade. These results indicate significant increases in understanding across all mathematical concepts in each unit from pre- to posttesting. Thus, Project M³ materials may help fill a curriculum void by providing appropriate acceleration and enrichment units to meet the needs of talented elementary students.

Hanushek, E. A., Peterson, P. E., & Woessmann, L. (2010). *U.S. math performance in global perspective: How well does each state do at producing high-achieving students?* Boston, MA: Harvard University, Kennedy School.
Abstract: This study compares the mathematics performance of high-achieving students in the U.S. to that of high-achieving students in 56 other countries. Results indicate that the percentage of students scoring at the advanced level in mathematics varies considerably among the states with no state doing well in international comparison. These percentages are well below those of many of the world's leading industrialized nations. Furthermore, the report suggests that the results are not influenced by a heterogeneous and difficult-to-educate population, nor by No Child Left Behind. Instead, it appears that schools are failing to teach students effectively.

Johnsen, S. (2005). Within-class acceleration. *Gifted Child Today, 28*(1), 5.
Abstract: This article describes ways teachers can accelerate the curriculum in their classroom by preassessing students and mod-

ifying their instruction, allowing them either to move through the curriculum at a faster pace or to provide in-depth learning experiences.

Johnsen, S. K., & Sheffield, L. J. (Eds.). (2013). *Using the Common Core State Standards for Mathematics with gifted and advanced learners.* Waco, TX: Prufrock Press.
Abstract: This guide provides classroom teachers and administrators with examples and strategies for implementing and differentiating the Common Core State Standards for Mathematics for gifted and advanced learners. Included in the booklet are underlying assumptions about giftedness and talent development, alignments across standards, research support, differentiated learning experiences, trajectories for talent development, implications for implementation and professional development, and multiple resources in the appendix.

Mann, E. L. (2006). Creativity: The essence of mathematics. *Journal for the Education of the Gifted, 30,* 236–262.
Abstract: For the gifted mathematics student, early mastery of concepts and skills in the mathematics curriculum usually results in getting more of the same work and/or moving through the curriculum at a faster pace. Testing, grades, and pacing overshadow the essential role of creativity involved in doing mathematics. Talent development requires creative applications in the exploration of mathematics problems. Traditional teaching methods involving demonstration and practice using closed problems with predetermined answers insufficiently prepare students in mathematics. Students leave school with adequate computational skills but lack the ability to apply these skills in meaningful ways. Teaching mathematics without providing for creativity denies all students, especially gifted and talented students, the opportunity to appreciate the beauty of mathematics and fails to provide the gifted student an opportunity to fully develop his or her talents. In this article, a review of literature defines mathematical creativity, develops an understanding of

the creative student of mathematics, and discusses the issue and implications for the teaching of mathematics.

(This article is a condensed version of Mann's dissertation, which can be found at http://www.gifted.uconn.edu/siegle/Dissertations/Eric%20Mann.pdf.)

National Academy of Sciences. (2007). *Rising above the gathering storm: Energizing and employing America for a brighter economic future*. Washington, DC: The National Academies Press.
Abstract: This document reports on the erosion of U.S. advantages in the marketplace and in science and technology. The report states that a comprehensive and coordinated federal effort is urgently needed to bolster U.S. competitiveness and preeminence in these areas so that the nation will consistently gain from the opportunities offered by rapid globalization. Four recommendations were made that focus on actions in K–12 education, higher education, and economic policy.

National Academy of Sciences. (2010). *Rising above the gathering storm, revisited: Rapidly approaching category 5*. Washington, DC: The National Academies Press.
Abstract: This document provides an update to the 2007 report by the National Academy of Sciences (see reference above).

National Center for Education Statistics. (2011). *The nation's report card: Mathematics 2011* (NCES 2012–458). Retrieved from http://nces.ed.gov/nationsreportcard/pubs/main2011/2012458.asp.
Abstract: This report presents the results of the administration of the 2011 National Assessment of Education Progress (NAEP) in mathematics and compares the results to previous years. It provides sample problems from the NAEP in each of the five content areas: number properties and operations; geometry; measurement; algebra; and data analysis, statistics, and probability.

National Council of Supervisors of Mathematics. (2011). *Improving student achievement by expanding opportunities for our most promising students of mathematics.* Retrieved from http://www.mathedleadership.org/resources/position.html
Abstract: This report highlights the idea that significant improvement in mathematics achievement over a sustained period requires addressing equity and expanding opportunities for the most mathematically promising students. A strong, diverse society has the right to demand that educators all look for mathematical promise in their students and seek to overcome the lenses of bias or low expectation that can cloud their vision. All students deserve a learning environment that lifts the ceiling, fuels their creativity and passion, and pushes them to make continuous progress throughout their academic careers.

National Mathematics Advisory Panel. (2008). *Foundation for success: The final report of the National Mathematics Advisory Panel.* Retrieved from http://www2.ed.gov/about/bdscomm/list/mathpanel/report/final-report.pdf
Abstract: The report presents actions that must be taken to strengthen the U.S. in mathematics. Although the U.S. possessed peerless mathematical prowess for most of the 20th century, without substantial and sustained changes to its educational system, the U.S. will relinquish its leadership in the 21st century.

Park, G., Lubinski, D., & Benbow, C. P. (2012). When less is more: Effects of grade skipping on adult STEM productivity among mathematically precocious adolescents. *Journal of Educational Psychology, 105,* 176–198.
Abstract: Using data from a 40-year longitudinal study, the authors examined three related hypotheses about the effects of grade skipping on future educational and occupational outcomes in science, technology, engineering, and mathematics (STEM). From a combined sample of 3,467 mathematically precocious students (top 1%), a combination of exact and propensity score matching was used to create balanced comparison groups of 363

grade skippers and 657 matched controls. Results suggested that grade skippers (a) were more likely to pursue advanced degrees in STEM and peer-reviewed publications in STEM, (b) earned their degrees and authored their first publication earlier, and (c) accrued more total citations and highly cited publications by the age of 50. The patterns were consistent among male participants but less so among female participants (who had a greater tendency to pursue advanced degrees in medicine or law). Findings suggest that grade skipping may enhance STEM accomplishments among the mathematically talented.

Reis, S. M., & Park, S. (2001). Gender differences in high-achieving students in math and science. *Journal for the Education of the Gifted, 25,* 52–73.

Abstract: Using data from the National Education Longitudinal Study of 1988, the researchers examined gender differences between high-achieving students in math and science. They found that there were more high-achieving males than females in this group, with far fewer female students in the science group. They also found that high-achieving males felt better about themselves than high-achieving females. Females who are high-achieving in math and science are more influenced than males are by teachers and families.

Robinson, N. M., Abbot, R. D., Berninger, V. W., Busse, J., & Mukhopadhyay, S. (1997). Developmental changes in mathematically precocious young children: Longitudinal and gender effects. *Gifted Child Quarterly, 41,* 145–158.

Abstract: Young children with advanced mathematical skill (N= 276) were followed for 2 years during kindergarten through first grade or first through second grade. Children were randomly assigned to a control group or a treatment group. Children in the treatment group participated in enrichment activities outside the school that supplemented the child's regular classroom program. Activities were problem-based and "constructivist" in nature. The students were administered the Stanford-Binet IV,

Key Math Test-Revised, Woodcock-Johnson Achievement Test-Revised, and the Word Problems Test. Gains occurred on three of the five math subtests, two of the three verbal subtests, and both visual-spatial subtests, with maintenance on the remaining three standardized subtests. Children who are advanced in math early continue to be advanced and may become more advanced relative to age peers once they enter school. Boys surpassed girls in performance. The intervention resulted in change in the quantitative domain but not the verbal or visual-spatial domains.

Saul, M., Assouline, S. G., & Sheffield, L. J. (Eds.). (2010). *The peak in the middle: Developing mathematically gifted students in the middle grades.* Reston, VA: National Council of Teachers of Mathematics.

Abstract: Good teaching is responsive to individual differences, tailoring instruction to meet the needs of individual learners. In gifted education, students need a curriculum that is differentiated (by level, complexity, breadth, and depth), developmentally appropriate, and conducted at an appropriate developmental level. This collection of essays from experts in the field addresses the particular needs educational institutions have in serving their gifted students. Topics include policy and philosophy, specific program models, supplemental materials and programs, knowledge and skills that teachers need in their work, international opportunities and possibilities, and equity. Many of the points raised are as valid for general education students as they are for gifted students. Many relate equally well to high school or elementary school. And many apply across the curriculum—not just to mathematics.

Sheffield, L. J. (2003). *Extending the challenge in mathematics: Developing mathematical promise in K–8 students.* Thousand Oaks, CA: Corwin Press.

Abstract: This book is a guide to the development of mathematical talent in students in grades K–8. The first chapter is about developing mathematical promise and considers characteristics of students who are mathematically promising, the goals of mathematics instruction, how to find and/or create good problems, models for increasing the numbers and levels of mathematically promising students, and assessment strategies. The remaining chapters offer suggested investigations into the following subject areas: number and operations, algebra, geometry and measurement, and data analysis and probability. Investigations offer activities at three levels of difficulty and are based on an open problem-solving heuristic.

Sriraman, B. (Ed.). (2008). *Creativity, giftedness, and talent development in mathematics*. Charlotte, NC: Information Age.
Abstract: Given the lack of research-based perspective on talent development in mathematics education, this book is specifically focused on contributions toward the constructs of creativity and giftedness in mathematics. It presents new perspectives for talent development in the mathematics classroom and gives insights into the psychology of creativity and giftedness. The book is aimed at classroom teachers, coordinators of gifted programs, math contest coaches, graduate students, and researchers interested in creativity, giftedness, and talent development in mathematics.

Van Tassel-Baska, J. (Ed.). (2004). *Curriculum for gifted and talented students*. Thousand Oaks, CA: Corwin Press.
Abstract: A collection of seminal articles and research from *Gifted Child Quarterly* are compiled in one volume, including articles on how to develop a scope and sequence for the gifted, the multiple menu model of serving gifted students, what effective curriculum for the gifted looks like, curriculum at the secondary level, and specific content-area curricula options in math and science.

Appendix C

Teacher Resources

Books and Websites

Chamberlin, S. A. (2013). *Statistics for kids: Model eliciting activities to investigate concepts in statistics*. Waco, TX: Prufrock Press.
Description: Perhaps the most useful and neglected content area of mathematics is statistics, especially for students in grades 4–6. Mathematical modeling is an increasing emphasis in many standards, such as the Common Core State Standards for Mathematics and the NCTM standards. In this book, teachers will facilitate learning using model-eliciting activities (MEAs), problem-solving tasks created by mathematics educators to encourage students to investigate concepts in mathematics through the creation of mathematical models. Students will explore statistical concepts including trends, spread of data, standard deviation, variability, correlation, sampling, and more—all of which are designed around topics of interest to students.

Institute for Mathematics and Education. (n.d.). *Illustrative mathematics*. Retrieved from http://www.illustrativemathematics. org.

Description: This website provides guidance to states and curriculum developers in implementing the Common Core State Standards (CCSS). The site provides a wide range of examples of mathematical work that students should experience if the CCSS are implemented as written. A variety of tools that support implementation of the standards are included.

Institute for Mathematics and Education. (2012). *Progressions documents for the common core math standards*. Retrieved from http://ime.math.arizona.edu/progressions/

Description: Describes the progressions of mathematical topics across several grade levels, which are based on the logical structure of mathematics and research on children's cognitive development. Each progression provides an overview of the topic followed by a discussion of each standard. Example problems are included.

Johnsen, S. K., & Kendrick, J. (Eds.). (2005). *Math education for gifted students*. Waco, TX: Prufrock Press.

Description: The book brings together the best articles published in *Gifted Child Today*. Given gifted students' accelerated and intuitive thought processes regarding mathematics, teachers need to design differentiated curricula and use strategies that increase the complexity and pace of instruction. The authors provide some specific strategies for both organizing a gifted program and teaching mathematically gifted students in either the general education classroom or in special settings. *Math Education for Gifted Students* offers information about how to differentiate for mathematically gifted students, as well as tried-and-true instructional strategies to employ, including tiered lessons, distance learning, and activities combining architecture and math.

Math Innovations—http://www.kendallhunt.com/mathinnovations/

Description: This series helps students develop the habits of mind that allow them to excel in the study of mathematics. *Math Innovations* is comprised of five units, each focusing on a specific topic to support the Standards for Mathematical Practice. These units provide teachers with flexibility and the opportunity for alignment and accelerated sequencing because the topics' order can be customized. Content also can be delivered digitally through eBooks that feature enhanced CCSS-aligned, whiteboard-ready activities for each lesson that can be accessed from school or at home.

National Council of Teachers of Mathematics. (2006). *Curriculum focal points for prekindergarten through grade 8 mathematics.* Retrieved from http://www.platonicsolids.info/focal_points_ by_grade.pdf
Description: Describes three curriculum focal points for each grade level and provides connections to guide integration of the focal points for a particular grade level and across grade levels. The focal points are clusters of the most significant mathematical concepts and skills at each grade level, Pre-K–8. NCTM states that the vast majority of instruction time should be spent on the focal points.

National Council of Teachers of Mathematics. (n.d.). *Real world math.* Retrieved from http://www.nctm.org/publications/ worlds/
Description: Online collection of previously published articles from *Mathematics Teaching in the Middle School* and *Mathematics Teacher* for middle grades mathematics teachers. The resource contains more than 150 articles, lesson plans, and activities that connect math to the real world and classroom.

Noyce Foundation. (2013). *Inside mathematics.* Retrieved from http://www.insidemathematics.org/
Description: A professional learning community for educators who want to improve students' mathematics learning and performance. The multimedia website features classroom examples of innovative teaching methods, tools for mathematics instruction,

video clips of mathematics instruction, and links to the CCSSM at each grade level.

Talent Searches

The list below describes several of the more well-known talent searches (defined in Appendix A). For a comprehensive list, see the Davidson Institute for Talent Development at http://www.davidsongifted.org/db/browse_resources_129.aspx.

Academic Talent Search (ATS)—University of California, Irvine (UCI): ATS is a testing program primarily for student in grades 6–10. It identifies students with extraordinary mathematical and/or verbal reasoning abilities and offers students an opportunity to improve testing-taking skills for the PSAT and SAT Reasoning Test. Website: http://www.giftedstudents.uci.edu/ats/

Belin-Blank Exceptional Student Talent Search (BESTS)—University of Iowa: BESTS uses above-level testing to identify students in grades 4–9 who need further educational challenge to fully realize their academic talent. BESTS students are eligible to participate in Belin-Blank Center precollege programs consisting of a range of summer opportunities as well as an academic-year program. Website: http://www.education.uiowa.edu/belinblank/Students/BESTS/

BESTS results are used to generate a comprehensive report. The Inventory for Decisions about Educational Acceleration and Learning (IDEAL) Solutions® for STEM acceleration is a web-based system that provides student-centered feedback to inform decisions about academic acceleration in math and science. Website: http://www.idealsolutionsmath.com/

The Carnegie Mellon Institute for Talented Elementary and Secondary Students (C-MITES): C-MITES provides academic summer and weekend programs to gifted students in kindergarten through 10th grade. The hands-on workshops emphasize exploration and investigation of advanced topics. They bring talented students together in a group, thus supporting their social and emotional needs and building a community of young scholars. C-MITES offers above-level testing for third through sixth graders, professional development for teachers, and informational workshops and publications for parents. Website: http://www.cmu.edu/cmites/index.html

Center for Bright Kids (CBK): CBK is a regional talent center located in Westminster, CO. In addition to the traditional talent search testing, CBK offers school- and district-specific trainings on partnerships to use above-level testing scores as an assessment tool for programs, as well as evaluation as part of an ALP. The CBK testing interpretation guide includes an addendum on "what to do next," with various models of talent development offered as a way to understand how to utilize scores. Website: http://www.centerforbrightkids.org

Center for Talented Youth (CTY)—Johns Hopkins University: CTY's talent search identifies advanced learners in grades 2–8 and serves as the bridge to CTY including its summer programs and online courses. CTY offers students greater academic challenges, interaction with intellectual peers, and teaching strategies designed especially for the gifted. Website: http://cty.jhu.edu

Talent Identification Program (TIP)—Duke University: Duke TIP identifies gifted children in fourth through seventh grades using above-grade testing and provides resources to nurture the development of these exceptionally bright youngsters. The program offers several resources to help participants use their above-level test results as a guide to maximize their education. After testing, participants receive a results summary that compares their performance to other talent search participants and offers suggestions for educational development. TIP's wide variety of educational programs, both residential and commuter, engage students through superb academic experiences. The Educational Opportunity Guide, an online directory, contains listings for schools, summer programs, and academic competitions across the United States and abroad, and the *Digest of Gifted Research* offers research-based information about raising and educating academically talented children. Website: http://www.tip.duke.edu/

Northwestern University's Midwest Academic Talent Search (NUMATS): NUMATS identifies through above-grade-level testing and serves students in grades 3–9 in Indiana, Michigan, Minnesota, Ohio, Wisconsin, Illinois, North Dakota, and South Dakota. NUMATS provides identified students with appropriately challenging programs and resources, and serves as a gateway to programs and resources for gifted students both at Northwestern University, as well as nationwide. Families and educators participating in NUMATS gain access to an online, password-protected toolbox. Through the family toolbox, students are offered invaluable test preparation materials and, after taking the test, scores are interpreted. Based on this analysis, academic recommendations tailored to the student are provided. Parents receive in-depth articles, engaging webinars, and continuously updated resources specific to understanding and developing the academic talent of their gifted child. Through the educator toolbox, schools with participating students receive face-to-face and online professional development and consultation. Website: http://www.ctd.northwestern.edu/numats/

Mathematics Contests

American Mathematics Competitions (AMC): AMC is dedicated to strengthening the mathematical capabilities of U.S. youth. They do so through a series of five national contests. In addition, AMC hosts an invitation-only summer program, which chooses the final six contestants for the International

Mathematical Olympiad Summer Program. Website: http://amc.maa.org/

Mathematical Olympiad Summer Program (MOSP): The MOSP prepares students for the International Mathematical Olympiad. Website: http://www.artofproblemsolving.com/wiki/index.php/Mathematical_Olympiad_Summer_Program

International Mathematical Olympiad (IMO): IMO is a world mathematics contest for high school students and is held annually in a different country. Currently, more than 100 countries participate. Participating countries send a minimum of six students. The contest involves several rounds of progressively more difficult competition where participants solve challenging mathematical problems. Website: http://www.imo-official.org/

MathCounts: Challenging math programs for U.S. middle school students. The competition program is a national coaching program that promotes mathematics achievement through a series of "bee" style contests. The club program is a math enrichment initiative that provides the structure and activities designed to encourage the formation of middle school math clubs. The Reel Math Challenge program is a competition in which teams of four students create a video based on one of the MathCounts problems. Website: http://mathcounts.org/

About the Authors

Susan K. Johnsen, Ph.D., is a professor in the Department of Educational Psychology at Baylor University, where she directs the Ph.D. program and programs related to gifted and talented education. She is the author of tests used in identifying gifted students and of more than 200 publications, including books related to the national teacher preparation standards in gifted education, identification of gifted students, and using the Common Core State Standards with gifted students. She is editor-in-chief of *Gifted Child Today*. She serves on the Board of Examiners of the National Council for Accreditation of Teacher Education, is a reviewer and auditor of programs in gifted education, is chair of the Knowledge and Skills Subcommittee of the Council for Exceptional Children, and is cochair of the NAGC Professional Standards Committee. She is past president of The Association for the Gifted (TAG) and past president of the Texas Association for Gifted and Talented (TAGT). She may be reached at Susan_Johnsen@baylor.edu.

Gail R. Ryser, Ph.D., is the director of the Testing, Research-Support, and Evaluation Center at Texas State

University. She is an associate editor for *Gifted Child Quarterly*. She is the author of several tests and has written numerous articles related to gifted education, mathematics education, and measurement. She is a coauthor of a popular series of books, *Practical Ideas That Really Work*, that includes research-based instructional strategies for students with exceptionalities. She may be reached at gr16@txstate.edu.

Susan G. Assouline, Ph.D., is the director of the Belin-Blank Center and a professor of school psychology at The University of Iowa. She is especially interested in academically talented elementary students and is coauthor (with Ann Lupkowski-Shoplik) of both editions of *Developing Math Talent*. She is codeveloper of *The Iowa Acceleration Scale*, a tool designed to guide educators and parents through decisions about accelerating students. In 2004 she coauthored, with Nicholas Colangelo and Miraca U. M. Gross, *A Nation Deceived: How Schools Hold Back America's Brightest Students*. She may be reached at susan-assouline@uiowa.edu.